LIFE IN CURSIVE

Staying connected, balanced, and inspired
through living a handwritten life

TRACY CARPENTER

RIVER BIRCH PRESS

Daphne, Alabama

Life in Cursive
by Tracy Carpenter
Copyright ©2021 Tracy Carpenter

Unless otherwise identified, Scripture is taken from: The Holy Bible, New International Version. Holman Bible Publishers. Nashville, TN, 1986. Copyright 1973, 1978 and 1984 by International Bible Society.

Scriptures marked NASB are taken from the *New American Standard Bible*, Copyright ©1960, 1962, 1963, 1968, 1971, 1973, 1975, 1977 by The Lockman Foundation.

Scripture marked NLT are taken from the Holy Bible, New Living Translation, copyright ©1996. Used by permission of Tyndale House Publishers, Inc., Wheaton IL 60189.

ISBN 978-1-951561-65-9 (print)
ISBN 978-1-951561-70-3 (e-book)

For Worldwide Distribution
Printed in the U.S.A.

River Birch Press
P.O. Box 868, Daphne, AL 36526

CONTENTS

ACKNOWLEDGMENTS

Writing a book has been a cathartic experience because it has caused me to reflect in such a deep and personal way. Not only have I drudged through every memory of such an unexpected trauma, but I have also looked back at all my time with God, and especially my childhood. I have been challenged on an all-new level to face my fears, dig deeper in the Word of God, and express myself clearly.

It is quite fun remembering all the wonderful people who took time out of their lives to make mine better. It is quite freeing to write all my innermost thoughts, ideas, and even stories on paper. The thought of producing something that may be around long after I am gone has taken me to new places in my existence. This book has allowed me special moments with the memory of my mother along with other beautiful remembrances I thought I lost touch with. Since this is my first book, it is a bit like having your first child: everything is new. And I must say, I have really enjoyed the process.

First and foremost, I have reserved my deepest gratitude for **Mike Carpenter**, my husband and very best friend. Not only is he a profoundly supportive husband who has absorbed incredible ups and downs with me, but also he has always helped me find my provision and my voice. His servant's heart, passion for children, and integrity make him an amazing husband and father. It has been decades since we first met and began dating, and I must say, if we both were single, and I knew everything I now know about him, I would still date him and marry him all over again. I always tell my kids, "You don't marry the person you can live with; you marry the person you cannot live without." That is exactly what I did, and to this day, I have not a single regret.

Second, I would like to thank my dad, **Tom Hicks**, who, from the beginning, said to me, "Are you going to be a leader or a follower?" He used to explain the difference in detail and say, "You will be one or the other, and it is your choice." Through every experience that brought me to adulthood, he would again say, "Are you going to be a leader or a follower?" It was his wisdom, love, and constant support that made me a leader. The funny thing is that now he asks my kids the same question. They already know what he is after; he is after their realization that they will be leaders too. My dad is my great friend, my confidant, and wholeheartedly a leader.

My earliest memories are of reading the Bible with my grandmother **Myrtle Syring**. She was my spiritual mentor, not to mention the kindest spirited person I have ever had the pleasure of knowing. She gave me so much good advice it would fill hundreds of books. She gave me a legacy of believing that godly character and honesty are more precious than anything else. She told me that what we have in material possessions is much less important than what kind of people we are on the inside and what we choose to do for others. She exemplified compassion at its utmost.

For my daughter, **Amanda Michal Carpenter**, our story always reminds me of how thankful I am for her. She is my lifesaver and a light to all who know her. I think a mother-daughter relationship is one of God's greatest gifts. I am so grateful for the years we were able to share together with Nana. She never, never, never gives up—not on anyone or anything. She has taught me firsthand how important it is to go the distance with every person and personality. Her merciful spirit and heart for the hurting are unsurpassed. She is my true friend. I look forward to all the memories we still have to make together!

For my son, **Adam Thomas Carpenter**, whose life from the beginning has been tumultuous and, some would say, chaotic, first with a problem pregnancy, to all the accidents, near drowning, and health problems. He has really taught me to pray and, ultimately, to hope. God has shown himself so mighty through him, and I am so thankful that he knows that. His creativity, passion, pure spirit, grateful heart, and genuine love for people never cease to amaze me. His ability to see the truth and wisdom in any given circumstance is definitely a gift from God. I absolutely love the way he celebrates life at every opportunity.

My uncle, **Robert Syring,** has been my constant supporter, especially in times of trial. There is nothing more precious than family. I am encouraged by his spirit and always in awe of his heart for anyone in need. His infectious laugh and love of people make him a very sought-after friend and confidant. Thank you for treating me like your daughter and always encouraging me forward.

I must, without a doubt, thank Pastor and dear friend **Steve Alley** for seeing things in me beyond any reason, and for most of all, helping me to find my God-breathed destiny. It was through his guidance and unconditional love that I was truly able to express fully what God had put inside of me. Thank you for teaching me how to write, always standing in the back of every lesson I ever taught to cheer me on, and most of all, for passing the honor of being children's pastor over to me with your blessing. All that God has done and will be able to do through me will always be, in part, due to you. I will never, ever forget where I came from.

Kerri DiMercurio gives me proof every day that true friendship does exist. Her passionate spirit and genuine compassion inspire and strengthen me often. She has a way of making me laugh, which I am sure could break windows somewhere. She would undeniably give up her life for her family. I know, without a doubt, God brought her into my life, and he continues to reveal new reasons why daily.

Bella Costello lived this story with me. She is a fighter! This is the girl you want to watch your back. Thank you for standing up for truth and justice for me and so many others. Your passion for life is not only refreshing; it's beautiful.

I thank **Annette Reynaud** for her friendship, unmatched wisdom, and consistently brilliant advice. She has a way of pointing absolutely everything to God—boy, do I love that about her. She sees the silver lining and always gives people the benefit of the doubt. She feels so deeply for others that there has not been one moment in life when I needed something from her, that she hadn't given it to me on the spot if she had the power to do so.

Without the guidance and encouragement of one **Mrs. Robin Eddy**, this book would not be what it is today. She always sees the best in me even when she is looking at the worst! I have said it before, and many will agree with me, Robin is perhaps one of the kindest people you could ever meet. She is patient and always self-sacrificing. I am lucky to have her as my dear friend.

When I think of **Eva Pena**, a flood of flashbacks instantly bombard my mind from writing hundreds of verse boards together to sitting with her for uncountable hours, brainstorming curriculum ideas. She immerses herself with her whole being into every project she ever dives into, including friendship! I am lucky to have shared memories both in ministry and in fellowship with her. Thank you for sharing life at every level.

I want to thank **Susan Sellers** for journeying alongside me through thick and thin, through highs and lows. Her love of people warms my heart. Her fierce loyalty, commitment, and servant's heart are always with me.

Carrie O'Connor Tucholski quite possibly uses the biggest words I have ever heard. Over the years, she has joined me in every cause I could possibly imagine. Through her support, encouragement, and enthusiasm, she has supported every scheduled event I have ever booked! Her work ethic, constant quest for adventure, and intense loyalty inspire me. Her famous last words are always, "What can I bring?"

Michelle Cyr gives new meaning to the word confidant. She walked me through this as only a brilliant therapist could. Her love of healing others, seeing others find peace, and helping others achieve wholeness has been a priceless gift to me. I can honestly say I would not be where I am today without her.

Jud Wilhite is perhaps the most passionate Christian I have ever met in person. I am thankful for every word of wisdom he has ever given me. I am thankful for every time I ever got to see him speak. It has been a great honor to collaborate and know him. Thank you for your unwavering support, friendship, encouragement, and for always keeping God front and center.

Bryan Klems, who edited the entire manuscript in an early draft, made too many contributions to count. He has taught me more than I ever wanted to know about passive and active voice and cheered me on. I am beyond grateful for his sound advice.

My literary agent, **Keith Carroll,** came along at just the right time. His experience and, in my case, patience proved to be a match made in heaven. Thank you, Keith, for your guidance, support, and commitment to see this story told.

Thank you, **Gloria Ratliff, Mindy Williams, Kim Ledbetter, Noelle Manahl, Jen Davis, Penny Syring, Jena Groff, Ciara Scott, Annelle Rosales, Harli Williams, Ashley Moore,** and **Lauren Mawhinney** for our God-designed moments together. I learned the true meaning of mercy, love, compassion, strength, joy, courage, hope, friendship, hard work, and gratefulness. I cherish every second.

And last, but by far not least, I want to thank everyone at **River Birch Press** for believing in this book and making it a reality.

It is so miraculous how God intentionally puts all kinds of different people in our lives with their unique personalities, gifts, and talents to teach us new and diverse things. God has, by design, made us interdependent, and I am profoundly grateful for that. I look forward to all of the remarkable things God will teach me over the next few years through the amazing people I mentioned above and perhaps new ones I am sure he will bring into my life.

FOREWORD

In times of trouble, we often ask, "Why?" We know God hears our question, but we seldom get an answer. Have you ever, through tearful eyes and a broken heart, cried out to the Lord and asked Him why something bad happened to you or your family? If you have experienced this depth of spiritual exhaustion, you're holding a book that will help you refocus and restore.

Tracy Carpenter has experienced a full life! She is a deeply passionate person who carries a clear calling and enjoys an intimate, personal relationship with Jesus. She has been blessed with a strong marriage and a happy family. She has gained wisdom through many years of ministry leadership. Yet, this blessed child of the King experienced a life-altering experience at the hands of someone who worked her way into Tracy's personal life and family to bring doubt, destruction, and deep emotional pain. Where was God? Why did He permit this to happen to one of His own?

We are told in scripture that "God's ways are not our ways," and that "His thoughts are not our thoughts," yet we wrestle with the question of "Why?" We know that God is all-powerful and all-knowing. We know that He loves us. We know that He is sovereign over all the earth, and yet He lets bad things happen to those who love Him.

For Tracy Carpenter and her family, all of the scriptures and encouraging words from others couldn't hold back the pain of being manipulated and pulled into a swirling tide of deceit. In the middle of it all, she wondered where God was and how this could have happened to her after all the years of service to Him.

The journey that God permitted her to experience was much like King David, Elijah, the Apostle Paul, and so many other godly people in the Bible. During the seemingly endless time of pain and discouragement, God was present only to bring her out of it a changed person. In the aftermath, Tracy began to long for "normal" again. She asked God to restore her faith in people and her faith in Him as her Father.

Throughout history, God has permitted bad things, bad

choices, and what we would define as evil to exist. We have all tasted the bitterness of the results of others' poor choices in our lives. We long for kindness, honesty, and faithfulness. We struggle with preventing the evil in the world from drawing us into its grasp and changing us. Yet, our heavenly Father begs us to "return to Him" and "draw near to Him."

After what she went through, can Tracy trust God? After what she experienced, can she let people into her life again? Will Tracy's detour from her positive, normal life help you face your own fears and reach out to grasp God's hand once again?

This book takes you on an eye-opening journey through the process of dealing with pain, doubt, and discouragement. You will encounter your own feelings and perspectives on life, the effects of others' sinful choices, and God's ultimate goodness. You'll discover the powerful, restoring peace of living *Life In Cursive!*

—*Steve Alley, Author of* Growing a Healthy Children's Ministry, *professor of child development at Grace College in Warsaw, Indiana, and a pastor of 45 years*

INTRODUCTION

Unceremoniously, a young woman, who worked for me, began a twisted web of lies and deceit spanning many months. She took advantage of my heart, compassion, friendship, professional career as a pastor, and my merciful spirit. The slow descent of my life began and continued to plummet until her diabolical plot exploded and every one of her lies uncovered.

Her schemes engulfed us like an all-consuming fire. Her game escalated, and she slowly and methodically worked to separate me from those close to me. It worked and I gradually went deeper and deeper into isolation and darkness. When all the truth came out, devastation surrounded me.

I hadn't seen my friends in months. My colleagues began looking at me like I carried a contagious disease. All my long-lasting relationships seemingly disappeared. As I sat in the aftermath, I found myself feeling separated from God, in shock, seeing a therapist, getting drug tested, grieving, fearful, confused, and full of doubt. Each day more truth unraveled, and as new details of her plan surfaced, less and less made sense. I slept for hours and hours, cried for days upon days. My mind shattered.

As the shock began to wear off, I started taking stock of what really happened. Left sitting in obscurity with PTSD, feeling alone and foolish, I grew very unsure of my emotions and myself.

It mystified me to know God so well for so many years and for some reason be unable to find him. It seemed like God left me, or I lost track of him somewhere along the way. I had an identity crisis with God. How could I have done all of this for God and this be the result? I knew so much about God. The God I knew doesn't leave people. The God I knew sees light in darkness. The God I knew always prevails. The God I knew spoke to me. The God I knew protected me.

Piles and piles of words from God in the past flew through my mind like a hundred socks in the dryer. I pulled out every word he had ever given me. I read every letter I had ever written down. Imagine sifting through beaches and beaches of sand for a single valuable and coming up empty over and over. I knew *what* I knew; I knew *whom* I knew, I even knew *why* I knew it. But for the life of me, I couldn't feel it. I couldn't feel anything.

Then I made one of the most important decisions of my life thus far. Feeling lost in the cracks, hidden from God, and in a firestorm of doubt, I could not see God but chose to believe he could see me. I chose to hold on to what God says, what I knew to be true, and not what I felt.

When I stepped out in faith, God showed up in a profound way. Relying on God for everything while embracing my vulnerabilities proved to be a very scary but amazing opportunity to really get to know God better. I am living proof of what God can do through his endless grace.

By reading about how God spoke to me, renewed my mind, restored my spirit, and led me through some of the hardest situations to ever hit my life, I pray you can be inspired, hear clearly from him, know how loved you are, trust him in a brand new way, gain new vision for your life, and find incredible power to breakthrough whatever is threatening to separate you from your God-given destiny.

This book is not about her and her story, however unthinkable. It's about what God has done through such evil and pain. It is about how I learned to stay connected, balanced, and inspired through living a handwritten life. This story is a call for all of us to live our lives in cursive, staying connected to who matters most—God. It is about what he did for me and what he can and will do for you.

For my mom

AUTHORS NOTE

Today is the day I sit in agreement with the Holy Spirit and follow His leading and say yes to pain. Today is the day I will write my story. I know better than anyone how much beauty awaits and how much beauty this story has in it. I also know that to get to the beauty, we must wade through the ashes. Some writers admittedly write books for themselves. This time, this story, this book is for you, my new friend, my reader.

I am a witness, by my life, to what a gracious God can do.

ONE

MY GLASS HOUSE SHATTERS

It felt like I was living on the inside of a glass house. I saw the world; I saw everything happening outside. From the inside, I couldn't touch, taste, or smell the outside. I especially couldn't be a part of it. Everything happening around me seemed like it moved in slow motion. I didn't know how to get out of it. I longed to be outside, but I remained trapped by something invisible.

I silently pounded on the glass, yearning to break free. Feeling like a failure, I lived inside this alternate existence without the ability to share anything with my friends or even some of my closest family. I did not recognize my life anymore; it no longer looked whole and healthy. Millions of tiny little pieces seemed to be all that remained.

At some point in our lives, we all seem to find ourselves in a glass house, feeling alone and abandoned. Some of life's circumstances can be terrifying. I can watch the news for an hour and feel my glass walls going up. Situations beyond our control threaten to take us from a life we love to a place we hate. Things can and do happen in our lives, which leave us frozen, grappling for understanding, and shattered in a million pieces. We can at times search every crevice of our heart and mind for our faith, only for it to elude us.

Maybe you get it. Maybe you too are looking through thick glass, trying to focus, and searching for meaning, balance, and something to connect you back to the joy you once knew. Maybe your glass wall went up with the loss of a baby, death of a loved one, a bitter divorce, or an unexpected traumatic event. Maybe all the letters of your life are dangling in the wind, disconnected, and out of balance.

There in my glass house, I stayed disconnected, detached, severed, separated, and divided from all I once knew to be reality. Life continued going on all around me and, as I watched from behind the glass, I slipped farther and farther away.

HYPERREALITY

An infinite number of reasons caused me to distance myself from the person I would have liked to be or once used to be. The disappearance happened involuntarily, unintentionally, and at times, I think accidentally. I lost myself. In a series of barely noticeable moments, I gradually distanced myself from the person I once passionately dreamed of becoming.

I know now the trauma I incurred directly affected my ability to reason. For that purpose and more, which you will learn about in the pages to follow, I had to climb my way out of a gaping hole in my life.

PAIN AND TRAUMA

This story happened at my church, in my ministry, right in the middle of my life. I ran free in a great season of gratefulness and progress; work challenged me, and my ministry goals flourished. Hope towered around me. God routinely spoke clearly to me, and I always responded audaciously.

Full of faith, I walked steady and secure in His Spirit. I spent hours upon hours reading, and my unquenchable desire for learning grew. Each day I woke to my own great expectations. I believe most viewed me as on-fire for God, content, full of creativity, and happy. My dreams lived in my reality.

Creativity always encircled me. I decorated my house constantly; I existed to find fresh new ideas. I spent innumerable hours on Pinterest and Instagram, searching for anything ingenious to get my hands on. Walking through Barnes and Noble and Anthropologie, while soaking up all the originality around me, qualified as a great day. I took long walks every day just to discover new things in nature and see the sky. I treasured innovation. I respected resourceful and imaginative people who worked hard and took risks.

I especially enjoyed going out to dinner and spending time with my family. I can remember walking carefree and full of hope with my husband, Mike, into my favorite restaurant. I ate up graphic design and particularly adored benchmarking other churches to gain inspiration. I loved quotes and philosophy. Writing freed me to be me.

A bottomless passion for social justice kept me up at night. I often thought and dreamt of how I might challenge injustice and make a real difference in people's lives. My heart and passion for social justice is one thing that never changed throughout this story; in fact, it still kept me up at night.

WHERE DID ALL THIS BEGIN?

I first noticed Emma running into the church. She wore a ministry approved t-shirt, so I instantly knew she served in the ministry I oversaw. Our weekend services had just gotten underway. I yelled, "Yay, Emma is here!"

Out of breath, she said, "Sorry, I'm late."

"No worries I'm so glad you're here!"

"Anytime, I love serving in the nursery!"

I quickly saw her big smile, affection for kids, and passion for serving. Soon I began to talk to her each time she helped in the nursery. The more I got to know her, the more I liked her servant's heart and vibrant personality.

She served faithfully at the church for more than four years before we eventually hired her to coordinate one of our children's ministry programs. She took to the work like fish to water. Whatever I threw at her, she eagerly took and ran with it. I once mentioned I needed to make a large graph for an important project, and sure enough, she handed me a complex graph within hours.

She had many talents, and each week, they seemed to be exploding like well-timed fireworks. She shined in ministry. Kids often fluttered around her, giggling and laughing as she played with them. She quickly began taking on new responsibilities, and it exhilarated me to see her flourish in leadership. She found a great fit in ministry and began lining out a beautiful career path. Everyone at work loved to see her walk through the door. She would rather die than miss work.

Once she shocked us all and came to work after minor surgery and spending the entire night in the hospital. Time flew by, and she quickly became a vital part of our staff team. Then abruptly, the Emma I had come to know seemed to vanish, and I didn't recognize her anymore.

After a year as a star employee at the church, Emma started dropping the ball. I noticed she began having difficulty sitting still, angered easily, and did not get along well with her co-workers. She began openly sharing about her troubles. She suffered from paralyzing anxiety, unrelenting insomnia, problems at home, fear, and many other trust issues.

We all worked near one another, and her struggles became obvious to the team. Each day I watched as Emma's foot tapped a million miles an hour under her desk. I waited for her to turn around before I asked her a question. I listened to see if she took deep breaths before I approached her. I learned early on in ministry how destructive eggshells in the workplace can be and began to recognize how dangerous Emma continuing to be on our team may be to the ministry.

On many occasions, I sat alone in my office and wondered how to get out of this, thinking, *Maybe I should move her to another area of ministry, or maybe I should decrease her hours a bit.* Then before I had a chance to address the current storm, her difficulties intensified.

Emma's life very clearly began circling the drain as her emotional problems worsened. I regularly walked in to work to find her head down, tears flowing, and unable to catch her breath. She walked into work one day wearing the same clothes as the day before, looking very disheveled. I asked her, "Emma what's going on?"

Emma replied, "I got kicked out of my house last night. I had to sleep in my car at the soccer field."

"What happened?" I stared at her with my eyes bulging. As far as I knew, she worked, didn't do drugs, went to school, and seemed very attentive to family and responsibilities at home. This information did not make sense to me.

When I questioned her as to the reason, she replied, "I'm not sure. My parents don't want me there anymore."

"Did you do something to make them upset?"

"They don't think I should be working here; they think I should be in school full-time."

"This seems sudden, whenever I talk to them they seem happy you're here. Are you sure nothing else happened?" Something is missing.

"Well, there is a lot you don't know about my parents. They're very controlling, and if I don't do exactly what they want at any given moment, they threaten to take my car and phone away and kick me out."

"What did they say exactly?"

Crying, she blurted out, "We argued for hours. They want me home every night for dinner at a certain time. They want me running all their errands. My mom wants me coaching soccer at the school where she works. My mom wants me on a diet. I'm twenty-two years old." She went on and on. "They want to know my every single move. If I don't come home one night for dinner, they go ballistic."

"Do you have your car?" I asked.

"Yes, my mom stole all my journals, tossed my room, and then took my car keys, but I found them, grabbed them, and left as fast as I could. It's my car. I pay for it!"

I saw her phone blowing up and instantly knew the significance of this day. At first, I saw a young girl fighting to spread her wings and greatly needed to be independent.

However, as things progressed, her need for attention and healing became very apparent. Because of her emotional issues, she had altercations with a couple of co-workers, and more than one of them stopped talking to her.

Sadly, as a result of her lies and scheming, one of the girls she didn't get along with quit. This girl that resigned had spent countless hours with our family. It saddened me to see her go. Looking back now, I believe Emma intentionally eliminated this girl from my life as an attempt to begin separating me from those I cared about.

Back then, my heart wanted to see Emma smiling and happy with a spring in her step. I desperately wanted to click the rewind button and go back to the Emma we all knew and loved. A dichotomy occurred. I wanted her feeling well, healed, looking forward to her future, and living her life to the fullest, while at the same time, I needed to protect the large ministry I oversaw. I hoped she would just snap out of it, and things could return to normal. As her pastor, I had a duty to minister to her; as her boss, I had an obligation to hold her accountable to her responsibilities.

A few weeks before Christmas, and about a month after Emma started falling apart at work, she asked if I would be willing to talk privately with her about some of the things she dealt with. I continued to notice how visibly distraught she appeared daily.

She seemed worried, distracted, and completely out of sorts. I agreed to talk with her, hoping to get to the bottom of things. I intended to move her in the right direction toward getting help and at the same time shield the ministry. I listened and prayed. I spoke to her about journaling, walking, crying, and lots of other coping skills I learned about firsthand some years back. A few days later, she sat on the couch in my living room, looked me dead in the eye, and asked, "Do you think something really bad happened to me?"

It took me off guard. She'd been over at my house helping plan our annual Christmas party, though she never confronted me about this before. While I knew issues existed, I had no idea what they could be, so I chose to listen before speaking.

"What do you mean?" I replied. I instantaneously wished for a subject change. I know I squirmed in my seat. Secretly, I believed something terrible must have happened to her based on some of the triggers I observed, but of course, who knew for sure? She freaked out in any dark room, she came unglued when anyone accidentally touched her neck, and terrible nightmares plagued her minuscule amounts of sleep.

I discerned something felt off; I just couldn't put my finger on it. At the time, lists bulged out of my head. The hundreds of people arriving at my house in a matter of days and the many things I needed to do in preparation crowded my thoughts.

"I mean do you think something happened to me, and it could be why I am having all these anxiety attacks and can't sleep?" And so it began.

"I really have no place commenting on your personal life or jumping to any conclusions."

"Ya, but what do you think?"

"Well, I think you're about to get married to a really nice guy whom you seem to love and loves you. From what I can see thus far, your relationship with your mom is strained, to say the least. Your dad may be controlling but does seem to care, at least based on what you have told me. It seems like the perfect time for you to work through whatever you're battling. It will help you to start your marriage off on the right foot. Yes, I think something happened, and it is time to figure out what, so you can heal and have a full life."

"I just want to feel better."

"You really need some help from a professional therapist to work through whatever is rearing its ugly head. Even if it takes time to do the work, it will be worth it."

I continued pastoral counseling with her, and she made an appointment with a local therapist. From what she told me, I thought Emma saw her regularly. She seemed ready and willing to do her work and take the necessary steps to get help. She appeared genuinely grateful for my help, and I left most of our conversations feeling hopeful.

I often wondered if all my training, education, life experience, and Bible knowledge really gave me the tools I need to counsel people. In my line of work, it's called pastoral counseling. However, on more than one occasion, I have felt very unequipped to handle the extent of dysfunction and agony people are dealing with. People need encouragement and prayer, that's for sure, but for some reason, it seems they always want and need more during these pastoral-counseling sessions. I never know what I am going to hear once I open the line of communication, and most of the time afterward, I wish I hadn't heard it.

TWO

WHAT'S A SAFETY?

"Why are you in the garage?" I asked Emma as the Christmas party music hummed through the air. The loud noise of our co-workers talking and laughing echoed behind us, making it hard for me to hear her response.

"I... I..." and she said no more. Her panic attacks were in full bloom. The garage provided a sanctuary so that no one could see her melting down—no one but me, that is.

Between the eleventh and the seventeenth of December, Emma kept seeing weird flashbacks of her past. They started with her in her bedroom at the age of six. Then sitting in my car on the seventeenth of December, she looked at me and said, "Tracy, I think something happened to me when I was six years old." The flashbacks continued for at least a week. Then she contacted her older brother, Brian, and began asking him questions about her childhood.

They began texting one another non-stop. I met Brian about a year prior at the church where Emma and I worked. During one of the church services, someone yelled, "We need a doctor!" A man seemed to be having a heart attack, and Brian came running out of the church and helped the unknown man until the ambulance arrived. Brian looked very young. He had a small frame, freckles on his face just like Emma, and his hair was neatly combed down. Having his shirt tucked in made him look very professional.

He looked way too young to be a doctor, although he had completed his residency. By the time Emma started questioning him about her childhood, he was quickly approaching his graduation from medical school. Soon he began texting me non-stop as well. He believed Emma had repressed memories. I remember hearing him say, "You are her safety."

I said, "What's a safety?"

"I believe Emma's repressed memories are coming to the surface. This happens when the person with repressed memories reaches a time or place in their life where subconsciously they feel safe."

I asked. "I make her feel safe?"

"Yes, her brain has identified you and your voice as a safe place where she can release and process her painful past trauma. Your voice might help bring her through whatever memories may come out." He had long medical dissertations about how this sort of thing works. Based on his experience, he explained how people with repressed memories revert to the memory in real time when they initially begin to recall it.

"How does this happen?"

"If something traumatic happens to a person or child, they sometimes bury the memory like it never happened. Later when they can process the enormity of what happened to them, and when they feel safe, the memory will come out."

"How will these memories come out, all at once?"

"The memories could surface all at once or in phases."

"How long will this take?"

"I'm not sure. The last thing I want is for her to get stuck in one of these memories and not be able to get back to the here and now. It's possible for the trauma to be so big and so difficult for her to process, she may not be able to find her way back to the present."

"What do you mean?"

"Essentially she could get stuck as a six year old or whatever age she is experiencing the memory. I did a stint in a psychiatric hospital in one of my residencies, and I saw a young girl get stuck like this."

This worried me. "I'm not qualified to do this."

"Since her brain has identified you as her safety, the best and safest place for her to be right now is with you. "

Deep inside, I disagreed. However, I trusted his medical opinion.

"Brian, you know she's living in her car, right?"

"I'm working on getting her a place to stay at a buddy's house. I'm gone constantly with work. I'm interviewing all week next week and won't even be in the state." He then asked, "In the meantime, can she stay with you?"

"Isn't there someone else she can stay with, don't you think she really needs to be with family?"

"I wish, I feel awful about this, but my other brother, Ralph, is knee deep in marital problems, and it will never work with her there." He tried to reassure me, "If it gets too difficult, you can text me and we'll try to figure something else out. I really want her to get these memories out; and with you, she has a chance to do it. I'll call my buddy tonight and try to work out all the specifics. I'll come out in the next couple of days to get her a storage container for all the stuff in her car and get her set up there."

Brian shared lots of their childhood memories with me.

"Tracy, when we were kids and I would tuck her in, she acted terrified. She used to beg me not to leave her alone in her room." He remembered some very late nights she ran into his room crying and pleading to stay with him. He seemed devoted to her.

"Brian, how old was she when you remember this?"

"Whatever happened must have happened around the age of six."

I asked, "Why."

"Because I noticed Emma's personality change, and the light just went out in her eyes." She too spoke of their close relationship often, and from the conversation I had with Brian, it seemed clear to me he loved her very much.

Over the next week or so, she slowly started to get pieces of her memory back. With each episode, she stared off in a trance-like state and appeared to be stuck in the memory. To help her process the images and trauma she continued seeing, he advised me on how to talk to her during and following each episode.

"What do I do when this happens?" I asked Brian.

"When she freezes up, gently touch her face and say her name over and over until she snaps out of it. She'll recognize your voice, and this will help her work her way through the memory and back to reality."

"Okay," I replied.

"Tracy, everything she's going through is normal, and it will pass as soon as the memories surface."

I began working harder with her brother in an attempt to get her a place to stay other than my home. In the beginning, I felt like he supported me. He texted me unwaveringly, wondering about her progress and asking me all kinds of questions, "How long did she stay stuck in the memory?" "How upset did she seem?" "What is she remembering?" I texted him about every memory she had the entire time, followed up with outlining what she remembered, and waited to hear from him about our next move.

THINGS WENT FROM BAD TO WORSE

About two weeks after I became her safety (I still hate that word), her memories began to surface in complete detail. Up until this point, her memories came out in fragments. She went into a daydream-like state, stared off seemingly pretty deaf to the outside world, while at the same time going through a memory.

She saw parts of things, heard disjointed conversations, and felt strong emotions of fear. I talked to her during a memory, but when she replied from inside the memory, she spoke to me as a child, or at whatever age the memories occurred. When inside these memories, she relived them as if they happened right then. For example, if someone pinched her in her memory, she cried out and grabbed her arm.

The recollections of memories became more frequent, well defined, and intense. The first repressed memory to surface in complete detail transpired right before Christmas. In this particular memory, she jolted, shrieked, and cried. I tried to keep talking to her, "Emma, how old are you?" "Emma, where are you?" "Emma, Emma, can you hear me?" She answered as though she knew me; at times, she even asked me to get her out and to please help her.

I questioned Brian on this repeatedly, and he continued to reassure me. The whole experience perplexed me. At one point, I went online and read all about repressed memories and other than varying opinions of whether they existed, most of his information tracked spot-on.

Explicit pictures burned in my mind. Vile descriptions and disgusting dialogue left me beyond shaken. According to some of her first recollections, her father picked her up during school on her seventh birthday. He took her to a motel about forty-five minutes away. She remembered the landmarks along the way, the color of the motel, and even the color of the carpet in the room.

When they arrived at the motel, he proceeded to molest her seven times, assault her, video her, and give her gifts, one for each year of her life. After she opened each gift, she had to thank him with a sexual act, which she described in gruesome detail. Every gift her father gave her came from Disneyland. When she eventually got home to her mother, Dad wanted Mom to believe Emma spent the whole day at Disneyland. I watched her as she talked like a little girl, begging her daddy not to hurt her. With every screech out of her mouth, I pretended not to be feeling anything even though heat flooded my body, my stomach turned, and I lost my breath.

I didn't want to make her feel worse by adding my issues to hers. Listening to this poor girl's story, I broke inside. This dreadful episode went on for hours. She sobbed uncontrollably as she went through each detail of the memory. She asked me questions such as, "What is he doing? Why is he doing this or that?" She described where every one of his body parts stood in relation to her body parts. During her recounting the memory, my face stung. I anxiously tried to hold back the tears. I wanted to bawl. The walls closed in on me. My mind raced with thoughts and questions—

How could a father do this to his child?

I am a children's pastor; I can't hear about kids getting hurt!

Please stop. Why me? Where was her mother?

How will I tell Mike [my husband] all of this?

I wonder if there are still blood trace elements in that motel?

I can't hear these things; I just can't hear these things!

I feel sick.

Where is her family?

I wish Mike were here! This has to stop soon!

This has got to be the last thing he will do to her.

We will get through this, and then I am texting her brother and having him come get her!

I'm done.

I feel so bad for her. Poor Emma...

I think he broke her arm?

How could this happen?

You can imagine what a seven-year-old girl might be going through. With an Oscar-winning performance, this very sick young lady acted it out. (I still can't believe she did it.) She twisted and turned, trembled and shouted, and then cried in pain. I called her name over and over again. She eventually woke up from her memory, where she acted and lived as her seven-year-old self, and began talking to me like her twenty-two-year-old self. When she came out of the memory, the memory no longer stayed repressed. She now had full knowledge of what had happened to her in the motel.

She then needed to talk through what she went through as a twenty-two-year-old. I went through it all over again, this time with twenty-two-year-old Emma. She grappled for understanding, "Why did my father do this?"

"Emma, I don't know. I am so sorry."

"He said he loved me while he did those things." She tried to understand what her father had done to her and why he did it. So did I. She attempted to reconcile the abusive father in her memories to the loving father she thought she grew up with. She went back over every deplorable second of that memory once again. She asked me a few times if I wanted her to stop. And, as much as I did want her to stop, I wanted her to heal more.

After this ended, we sat there staring at one another, completely exhausted. Emma took a Xanax and fell asleep. I didn't. The images replayed in my mind like a movie I couldn't pause.

My husband, Mike, eventually came upstairs, turned the corner to our room, and asked, "Well, how did it go?" His eyes were red from lack of rest, and his dark hair was messy. I wondered if he just woke up. It turned out that he had decided to wait downstairs while Emma and I talked. He wanted to give Emma her privacy.

I cried, shouted, and in shock, began uttering things and talking to myself. I did not want one more second of this. I frantically wanted to go backward. I sat on my bed shaking my head over and over, wishing this never happened. I must have seemed like a blithering idiot. Mike didn't flinch. He listened patiently, and then after about thirty minutes, he too sat in shock and horror. I can still remember looking in his eyes while we sat on our bed, both heartbroken, shaking our heads saying over and over to one another, "How did this cruelty happen?" We both felt so sick and sad for Emma.

From our perspective, she desperately needed to confide in someone. We thought she wanted to share the many occurrences of her unbelievable abuse with a caring person who wanted to listen and help her through it. I contemplated over and over what to do. I did not want to continue or even be her pastor. I simply wanted this whole nightmare to stop. I wondered how to make this all stop. *How do I get out of this? How do I get her to leave? How do I protect my mind from these images?*

My mind frantically searched for reasonable, compassionate answers to all of these questions. Then I kept thinking that if she endured this trauma, the least I could do was listen. I felt guilty for wanting to abandon her. So I listened and listened and listened. This marked the day she became a wounded seven-year-old little girl who needed my love.

JACK AND THE BEANSTALK

I resolved myself to become more self-sacrificial. I heard every relevant Scripture and sermon in my head. Proverbs 3:27, "Do not withhold good from those who deserve it when it's in your power to help them," echoed in my mind.

"Get out of the boat," John Ortberg's famous words came rushing to my mind. I heard the libraries of Christian books on my bookshelves yelling at me to get out of my comfort zone and help someone. As much as I screamed no inside...NO! I fought what I felt and resolved not to let my flesh win.

I declared my fears and weakness wouldn't eclipse the needs of this lost person. Emma belonged in my flock, and I saw my calling to pastor her.

Be shepherds of God flock that is under your care, watching over them—not because you must, but because you are willing, as God wants you to be; not pursuing dishonest gain, but eager to serve (1 Peter 5:2).

How does a person who loves God walk away from a hurt child in a heap on the floor, covered with a mountain of abusive memories?

I heard the song "Broken Vessels" by Hillsong playing in my head. The verse, "Raising up the broken to life," kept spinning in my heart and mind. I wanted God to set her free and allow God to raise her to new life. I saw myself as a broken vessel, and I knew God had set me free so many times. I saw this as my turn to sacrifice, my opportunity to be eager to serve.

I knew in my weakness, God would show his strength. I had a great life, childhood, and a beautiful family while she didn't. I had plenty of support, and I assumed God must have put her in my flock for a reason.

I felt that she needed someone to go the distance with her. If God called me to help her, he surely had relief, support, and provision ready for me. I knew God enough to know that if he stood right there in that moment, he would scoop her up and comfort his broken child. Aren't I supposed to be the hands and feet of Jesus?

Knowing what I did, I took an obedient step in faith to do what I comprehended would honor God. I decided to stay the course with her no matter how grueling it would become. I wanted to be eager to serve by setting my fleshly feelings aside and standing up in Christ, ready and willing to do his work.

If this had happened to me and I sat in the aftermath of such brokenness, I hoped and prayed for the outpouring of someone's love and support. God is love, and he loved broken people, so I ultimately decided to sacrifice myself to love her.

When we find ourselves broken and wrestling for understanding, we try to reason our way forward. Looking back, I thought I was doing the right thing. I think for many of us who find ourselves full of fear, regret, and even pain, we often blame ourselves first. Some trauma has no reason.

We can't reason the unreasonable. Serial killers, child molesters, horrific accidents, cancer, and famine have no reason. Yet we try. The good news is that even when we make the wrong choice and receive devastation and despair as a result, God sets us right again. Sometimes we get disoriented trying to do the right thing. Thankfully, God journeys with us no matter how lost we find ourselves.

Whatever moment brought you inside your glass house, there is another moment waiting to bring you out. I believe fresh air and insight, inspiration, peace, and balance are right in front of you.

God finds us.

THREE

UNRAVELING OF ME

More memories of Emma's assaults by her father surfaced daily. Hundreds of accounts of brutal force, blood, fear, and panic rose around us. The viciousness took place everywhere. No place was off-limits for his assaults. It seemed that he waited around every corner and watched for every opportunity to take what he wanted and steal her innocence forever.

She pleaded with me not to tell anyone of the inconceivable cruelty she had endured. Everything petrified her, especially her father. Her father and mother attended the church where we both worked, and if his name even came up, she shook, her eyes went blank, and she disappeared. The floodgates of her memories opened, and she soon realized others besides her father had abused her.

She recalled one such incident at age seven by a friend of her father's named Reese. After her dad put her to bed, she heard a loud knock at the door, and her father invited a man in. He greeted the man with a polite hello and called him Reese. In a few moments, Emma's father led Emma into the living room. Her father introduced her to Reese. She remembered him from her father's work.

Her father left the house and Reese whispered all kinds of foul absurdities in her ear while he did unspeakable things. His heaviness caused her to stop breathing and pass out multiple times. After he finished, he got up and put his clothes on while she lay there, barely breathing. Her father reentered the scene to find Emma nearly dead and greeted Reese without even checking on her. Emma's father walked Reese to the door, at which time Emma saw Reese hand her dad money.

Her father said, "Thank you." Then her dad came to her, "I am so sorry, Emma." He walked her back to bed but not before he cleaned every bit of blood off of her. He redressed her and gave her medicine before tucking her back in bed. My mind swirled with new levels of confusion. He thanked that man for hurting his daughter? Why would her father do this? Was he videoing this? He is sick.

Reese and others emerged in and through her recollections, and soon many more men and women attacked her. Her memories got more overt as they developed. The blood, the torture, and the sheer boldness of the people hurting her astounded me. Then the shock of realizing her father was in the sex trafficking business hit us all.

She started having a memory of herself at seventeen years old in a strange place with lots of men around her. Each new memory opened different windows into revelations and exposed more truth as to what happened to her. I cared deeply for her and slowly died inside with each revelation.

As she went through this memory, she realized they used her pain to make a movie. Reese appeared not only in Emma's childhood memories; he also appeared in the more recent ones. During this memory, Reese and others beat, assaulted, and verbally degraded her. When the new disclosures of this type of obscenities, porn films, and her age came out, everything changed.

"Emma, how did your father get away with this? You're seventeen!" I asked

"He flew me to New Orleans to see a friend for my high school graduation present, and instead of getting to visit my friend, he drugged me and took me to a residential house."

"Emma, can you see the front of the house? Can you see the address?"

"Yes, I can."

"What is it?" She told me the address, and I wrote it down.

"Tracy, I didn't want to do any of this." Emma sat on the floor hugging my legs, sobbing as she told the story of many men.

And then she cried out a name—Nicolas.

One of the men in the house the day of the filming bore the name Nicolas. He showed kindness to Emma and did not hurt her when given the chance. He whispered the words "baby girl" in her ear and seemed to know her. She had no concrete memory of him but alluded to having feelings for him. During this memory, Nicolas told her to see beyond the words, which made no sense to her or me. He comforted her. Though unsure why, she believed he had tried to protect her.

Inside the house, the men took her from room to room to film different scenes. What an awful day for me. During these particular memories revealed in my living room, I took pages of notes as she uttered them, and passed her the notepad when she needed it. She took the pencil from me and wrote down names, vile language, and ugly references.

She drew tattoos on the paper that she saw on the men as they came into view of the camera. I took notes during most of her incidents and held on to all of her drawings.

This memory seemed to go on forever, and the sheer evil disturbed my heart. During the movement from room to room, Emma said she saw a baby girl. She heard the baby cry and carry on during her scenes. She heard Reese yell at Nicolas, "Nicolas, keep your baby quiet!" The baby belonged to Nicolas and based on her memories, the little girl seemed to be about a year old. They called the baby by the name of Jane.

Her brother Brian, the resident doctor, continued helping me and assisting her. He finally came and took her to his house for the weekend. Initially I felt relief, only for the relief to be stolen away within hours.

Emma locked herself in the bathroom, and Brian texted me the whole time, trying to find a way to get her to come out. He believed she got stuck in a memory and needed my voice to get out. After this weekend, he recognized how much she struggled, and he decided to try to come and stay with her near me.

As the weeks marched on, my husband and I continued speaking to Emma about turning her father in to the police to be punished for what we now were sure he had done to her. She had addresses, drawings, and clear memories. For all we knew, he never stopped doing it. For all we knew, the baby named Jane grew old enough to be subjected to the same appalling violence and abuse Emma had experienced. For Jane's and other innocent children's sake, my husband and I felt we had to do something to stop these crimes. We sat with Emma and begged her, "Emma you have to tell the cops what you know."

"I don't know," she replied.

"Emma, what about Jane? She would be around six now—the same age you were. Emma, we must save Jane."

"Tracy, I'm scared."

"I know. Think of Jane Emma."

She finally agreed to talk to her brother Ralph about everything. Her brother Ralph had studied and finished law school but had not yet passed the bar exam. Brian filled Ralph in daily on the facts and kept him up to date as the memories unfolded. They felt sick and disgusted at what their father had done, and they choose together to fight back. After Emma reached out to Ralph, he began texting me.

A bit of a hothead, full of colorful language and vehement about seeing his father arrested, Ralph never held anything back in his communication. I appreciated his authenticity, but cussing is not my thing. God worked that out of me years ago. My kids have never even heard me say a cuss word, and here I sat inundated with F-words and every other word texted every second.

For days he pressured her to go to the cops and tried to persuade me to get her to go to the cops. He asked me to take pictures of all the notes and drawings I had and send them to him. He planned on building a case against his father and assembling a file for law enforcement.

Ralph went to a local Christian school growing up, and there he had met a close friend named Don, whose dad now worked in law enforcement. Ralph, knowing this man's trustworthiness and credibility, decided to call Don's dad personally. He gave him a brief explanation of the happenings with Emma and asked to meet with him to gain advice.

Don's dad agreed and made plans for them to meet him right away.

One afternoon while her family were out of the house, Emma snuck into her parents' house, opened the safe, and grabbed her father's computer, flash drives, and whatever else she could get her hands on. Then she took those items along with her drawings and all my notes, and traveled to Los Angeles to meet with Ralph and Don's father, Agent Johnson.

Agent Johnson (not his real name) worked in the child trafficking division of the FBI, pretty high up in the organization. He left the meeting thankful they decided to meet with him. He let them both know to expect it to take a few days to gather all the information off the computer and strip all of the devices, but he would call as soon as he knew anything.

A few days passed. As I sat at my desk, I heard Emma's phone ring. Agent Johnson's number appeared on the screen. She said, "It's him!"

"Answer it!"

She panicked. She stood up, grabbed the phone, and ran outside to the front of our offices. I could hear her. "Ya...ya...ok...ya...I will." Then she hung up.

"What did he say?"

He said, "They finished and want to report to me what they found on all of my dad's stuff."

"When?"

"Tonight at eight."

We got home and waited anxiously. Emma's phone rang precisely at eight. Agent Johnson asked her to get a pencil, and I watched as she wrote down the findings. They found more than 800 counts of pornography on his computer, along with explicit photos of her. They told her one of the drives she provided held a video of the entire incident when she turned seven years old. He had filmed every second with her in the motel. Finally, it seemed that we got him!

IS THE IMPOSSIBLE POSSIBLE?

Soon we found out they discovered more on the computer than they initially thought. Agent Johnson asked to meet with Ralph again. At this meeting, Agent Johnson told Ralph that some years ago, the agency received a letter from a man named Nicolas. For years Nicolas had sent letters, giving the FBI tips on where to find kids that the organization sold and trafficked.

In addition to what they found on Emma's father's computer, these letters made them believe there might be a connection between this Nicolas and the one Emma knew. Agent Johnson showed Ralph pictures of Jane and felt that maybe Jane was Emma's child. When Emma told agent Johnson about Reese, Nicolas, and baby Jane, Agent Johnson thought he knew Nicolas but wanted to be sure.

One of the letters Nicolas sent to the FBI said that when Jane's mother came forward, they could promise her protection. He planned to give them incriminatory evidence on the organization he worked for and testify against all of them to get Jane home to her mother. The FBI thought Nicolas fit the profile of a boy kidnapped many years ago. They believed they had found his parents and thought they knew his real identity, but so far, they deemed it too dangerous to pull him out of the organization.

There seemed to be no way for Nicolas, now an adult, not to face criminal charges for his actions as an adult unless he worked with the Agency. So over the years, he gathered information from the organization in hopes of one day being truly free from them. Could Jane be Emma's baby? At this point, Emma had no recollection of having Jane.

It became evident that Emma was involved in something much extensive than anyone knew. According to Agent Johnson, if their hunch turned out to be correct, Emma remained involved in one of the largest child pornographic rings.

I continued my support and encouragement. Agent Johnson called often, and the FBI began putting together the many pieces they had. I observed her making a trip to the judge's chambers and on the phone a lot with what we thought to be detectives and psychotherapists. Emma's memories kept evolving, and as her memories flowed, more and more proof piled up against Reese and many other criminals as well.

The investigation soon turned up valuable information substantiating her involvement in a massive child porn ring called Baby Girl. This ring, which her father belonged to, marketed her in Las Vegas and flew her around the country to traffic her to many men and women.

I thought hearing her relive the memory of her seventh birthday classified as the worst night of my life. Now I knew that night to be only a drop in the bucket compared to the flood of horror now pouring on my head. My gut-wrenching pain for her situation and the call on my life to help people collided. As the collision continued, it crushed me.

The FBI soon contacted Nicolas and got DNA from Jane. I remember talking to Emma in my office, "Emma, is Jane yours?"

"She can't be," Emma replied.

Agent Johnson gave us Jane's birthday, so we looked at my large calendar, and I asked her questions like, "Where were you the weekend Emma was born?"

"I played soccer all the time; there is no way I played pregnant!"

"I know but look at all these things you have remembered that we never thought possible."

"I get flashes but nothing makes sense."

"I remember I gained weight, and my mom put me on a diet that year."

"Do you remember anything else?"

"Yes."

"Like what?" I asked.

"I remember my dad took me away to a soccer tournament that weekend!"

DNA results came back a few days later, and they proved beyond a shadow of a doubt, Jane's DNA made her Emma's child. *Was this true? Did Emma really have a baby?* Emma's shock initially overwhelmed her, but in time, she recalled every detail of having her. Dad took Emma away to the mountains. A doctor employed by the ring induced her, and after the baby arrived, they drugged her again. She remembered seeing the baby but never holding her. She cried in her memory as the ring took Jane.

After finding out Jane belonged to Emma, Nicolas worked diligently with Agent Johnson and the other agents on a plan to get him out from under Reese, organized crime, and the child pornography ring. They busted Reese in the act, and then Nicolas turned in all the proof he had to the police, and they put him and Jane under witness protection.

They ran the DNA on Nicolas and found him not only to

be Jane's father but also was once a six-year-old boy named Owen Timothy who was kidnapped in Haiti when his parents traveled there on a mission trip. They got in touch with his parents, and they went with him into the witness protection program.

Nicolas, now Owen, emailed us and told us all about the beautiful reunion. My first email from Owen:

Tracy,

I am sorry this is the only way I have to contact you, but I will take what I can get. Sorry this email has arrived so late, but I had much to say and decided to finish it during my layover. I am excited and look forward to the day I am able to share my daughter with you and be able to sit down and have an actual conversation with you about the things I have gone through.

You cannot imagine the things I have heard, seen, and done having been raised inside of a child pornography ring. My story is not one of sadness, though, for it is filled with hope and a God who never left my side. Please don't mistake any of this as me saying it was at all easy for it was not. I had many moments of weakness, doubt and plenty of self-blame.

I want to share a little of the story of Nicolas with you because it's a story of hope. I was taken shortly after my sixth birthday from Hinche Haiti while on a six-month mission trip with my parents. I have never felt the kind of fear I felt on that day and I will never forget that feeling. Many days later I was back in the United States being handed to a man and told he had adopted me as his son.

I will spare you the details of my first night with Reese but at the time I would have rather died. My first day as Nicolas, I thought was the worst day of my life, until I met Emma. You see I lived with Reese and crying every night feeling completely hopeless, but a year had gone by and I had accepted my life with no hope. When I was seven Reese drove us to a park where I met this little girl, when I saw her I knew she had been touched, she was like me but there was something about her. I will never forget her in her little blue dress with her curly dirty blonde hair pinned back with a bow.

When she looked at me I saw hope and when she talked to me I heard a future. There was light in her eyes that I had lost in my own. We sat on the swings and she told me about what had happened to her and I told her my story as well. This little girl who didn't even know me promised to save us one day and in return I promised to marry her. We were children who had gone through some of the worst trauma a child could so please understand I do not hold her to this promise.

This little girl gave me back a hope I never thought I would have again. Talking to her on the swings was the first time I heard from God. Let me explain why this is what I consider to be the worst day I had as Nicolas because I know you would think I would consider this the best.

This was the day I realized I wasn't the only child going through this and I had never experienced that kind of sorrow. I saw this little girl who had lost herself but still had a glimmer of hope in her eyes and I fell in love with her. From that day forward I continued to hear from God and my hope returned. Everything I endured was still very hard and painful but I had hope and hope can do amazing things for the soul.

It was not until I was sixteen that I saw Emma again. When her dad hired, me I didn't realize whom I would be required to be with. When I walked into the room and saw Emma lying there I knew instantly I would not hurt her that day. When we went into the bedroom and talked I knew she didn't remember me. She had gone through hell but there was still that glimmer of hope in her eyes. That day was the first time either of us knew that sex could be a good thing and it was the first and only time sex has meant anything to me.

I found out about six months later that Emma was pregnant with my child. Reese immediately started making a plan to get the baby but I stepped in. I knew Reese didn't want a baby but he wanted a little girl he could use at his disposal. I made a deal that he let me raise my daughter until she was six before he could touch her. I said six because I had already known Emma would be back before Jane was near the age of six.

From the time Jane was placed in my arms I took pictures. I wanted Jane to have the life Emma would have given her and I wanted to make sure Emma saw every single moment of it. I must admit my fashion sense had to adapt to having a little girl. I raised Jane with the expectation that one day I would hand her over to Emma and never look back. When I saw Emma again when Jane was six months old I knew once again that Emma had forgotten. She didn't remember but I knew she would and I knew it would take time.

I was willing to wait because I already knew from God that Emma would be the one to save us. For sixteen years I was forced to do the vilest of things, forced to disgrace women, filmed, and beaten but today, I am grateful. Today was worth the wait and Jane was worth the pain.

Never once has Jane been touched, never once has she seen any act of sexual nature, and never once has Jane been called baby girl. The men in the organization use baby girl any time they are doing something to a young girl and continue it through their entire life. They try to implant the words in such little minds. They continue to use it every time so these little girls feel owned by those words. It's a mind thing they have used for many years.

When we were in New Orleans, I tried to whisper in her ear those words so she would know I meant no harm when I said them. Emma has far more potential than she can see right now. She has a purpose far greater than any of us can even imagine. You as well have a major role in where she goes from here in her life and it's a far greater role than you can begin to imagine.

I hope you stick this through and believe strongly in Emma. Your name signifies that you have God's protection and I truly believe that. God speaks to you and the same God speaks to me. Sticking this out will be hard but sometimes the right thing isn't always the easy thing. Remember, Satan can't break your spirit of you don't let him.

Now lastly I want to give you some hope today because I feel you need it, I want to tell you about my reunion with my parents. My mom cried for four hours and wouldn't take her eyes off me. She feels Jane is her second chance and coming into her life at the same age I was taken from her is not an accident. She told me about the pain and heartache she felt all these years, and it was very hard to hear but nothing that surprised me.

She wanted to touch me and hold me, and if it wasn't me, then it was Jane. My dad was in disbelief of what he was seeing and couldn't wrap his mind around it. Last night Jane asked for us to all pray together before bed. She prayed:

> "Jesus, thank you for Daddy and new grandma and grandpa. Help us see Mommy soon, and I miss Tracy. I love you. Amen. Hallelujah. Praise the Lord."

> God is moving, so be ready.

I sobbed as I finished his letter.

After Owen's rescue, the FBI determined Emma needed protection as well. She rapidly turned out to be a crucial witness in a very large case.

Each evening at eight, she had a call with a very discreet Special Forces branch of the FBI. Agent Johnson sat second in command of this branch, and he made all contact with Emma. When they called, we had to clear our house of visitors and be very quiet. She sat in my living room for hours each night talking to them.

They played voices of men they thought to be involved, and she listened and tried to identify them. As she heard these voices, she often went into shock, and it took a very long time for me to get her to come back to reality. These meetings sometimes lasted until one or two in the morning. We heard her end of the conversations, though I often wished we didn't.

Her incessant need of me engulfed me. Her distorted revelations were all I could cope with. With each passing day, my exhaustion grew, and my wisdom withered. I hunkered down like when a kid had the flu or a huge project due at school. I took on a single focus, and all I could see was what was within that lens.

I was so focused on what I had to do to survive that I lost focus on the things that escaped my view. Out of sight, out of mind. I wasn't grocery shopping or planning meals. I wasn't decorating my house, planning a party, or going out to dinner with my husband. I stopped dreaming and could no longer see my life in terms of my future. I did not see my friends or family. The landscape of my life blurred.

Finally, I saw through the lens clearly; and the picture of my life as I knew it was gone.

OUT OF BALANCE

When we find ourselves out of balance and out of control, we tend to bargain with ourselves. We promise ourselves this is temporary or for a good cause. We tell ourselves we must do this for work or that for family. We sometimes justify being out of balance. Maybe we think we are too important, or perhaps we just can't break away from an exciting project. In this case, I kept telling myself this is for a short time, she needs us to help her, and soon this will be over. My simple needs like groceries and fun seemed minuscule compared with saving hundreds of kids' lives and protecting her.

I realize now how strategic Satan can be and how focused he is on stealing our joy and peace. I see clearly now how patient he was and is. I also see now how dearly God loves us and how fiercely he will come to our rescue.

FOUR

ARE WE SAFE?

To keep Emma safe, the agents approved only a small list of individuals to know about the case. My husband made the list, as did a couple of other people. They initially added Kara, a friend and co-worker, and her daughter Bailey so they could run cover for Emma at work. In the beginning, these two both loved and helped Emma. Unfortunately, they didn't stay in the loop the whole time. Emma turned on them, ostracized them from the case, and isolated them from me.

They instructed everyone on the list not to share any of the information we now had with anyone else. They made it crystal clear to us what to expect if we shared anything. They threatened prosecution and possible detainment if any one of us breached the circle of trust. They did not want to suddenly uproot Emma from her life. They felt to take her to witness protection might bring undue attention to her and possibly tip off the ring to her involvement.

Within days, twenty-five agents moved into two homes in my neighborhood and began watching our every move. They began building the case against Reese and hundreds of others who were now involved. Emma finally met her daughter and began limited visits with Jane. Emma had pictures of Jane. Jane had big blue eyes, the same dirty blond hair as Emma, and the cutest smile you ever saw.

Owen continued to email often and kept us updated daily on Jane's adventures. Having Jane safe meant the world to us. If only this is where it ended. They put us under constant scrutiny, and our separation from everyone we knew and loved truly began.

FEELING TRAPPED

Soon after this suffocating isolation began, one thought after another spun in my mind, smothering me.

I am stuck in my house being watched by the FBI. Seriously?

When did they bug my home and office?

I say something in my office, and I get a text response from law enforcement.

They communicate with me even if I change my driving pattern.

They are checking my car for tracking devices.

The FBI is delivering my groceries, staking out my house with cameras, leaving me notes, texting me during the wee hours of the morning, and integrating themselves in every aspect of my life.

They are reading my texts.

They know my passwords to my computer.

They know family information.

Do these poor guys get to go home?

How do I talk to my husband?

Everyone is asking me how I am—I feel so dishonest.

Have they been in my house? Yes! They have!

I see flashlights in the backyard every night—who is back there?

At one point along this voyage of deception, Emma slept on my couch. My husband and I sat in nearby chairs. At one point my husband received a text:

From: Agent Johnson
My witness has a bloody nose, will you please help my witness?

We looked over, and sure enough, her nose bled, and blood ran down her face while she slept. How did she do this? Another time my husband drove around a corner with her in the back seat, and he received a text saying, "Please slow down with my witness." They watched us, or at least we thought they did. Afraid to even blink, we carefully watched our every step with her.

Our desire for justice grew right along with her stories. We longed to see her whole again. We obeyed everything the FBI told us. We tried to make the best of it, but the information coming out of her and the information I needed to document grew more horrific each day. I recorded senseless murders of children and where they buried them, countless instances of violence, and detailed accounts of torture.

In some of the FBI searches, they found safes. Inside them, they found videos of Emma in torture rooms. I went through each one of these memories with her one by one.

They branded her, stabbed her, suffocated her, and even squeezed lemon juice in her eyes while brutalizing her, all for the camera. They staple gunned her legs, burned her, cut her back, and poured acid on her. They hung her from her feet. You name it; they did it. So many things she described I had never heard of in my entire life.

One afternoon Emma went into a memory in a torture room. They took her to these rooms to film brutal scenes for films and also for their own personal enjoyment. She started moving her arms, and it became apparent they strapped her down. She screamed out in pain. I tried saying her name and shaking her, but she did not snap out of it. Then all of a sudden, she froze and started begging her mother to stop.

I said, "Emma, Emma what's happening?"

She cried and cried, and then she spoke to me from her childlike state, "Why is my mommy hurting me?

"What?"

"Mommy, stop!"

"Emma, what is she doing?"

"She's hurting me."

"What is it Emma?"

"I'm bleeding."

"Are you sure it's your mom?"

"Yes, Mommy says I'm a bad girl."

She proceeded to share the details of this encounter, and as she shared, I realized her mother's involvement. Her memories came running out after this one opened the door. She said her mother worked for the organization. She took pictures of Emma and ran the operation of kidnapping foreign kids and getting them to the United States for trafficking.

Emma's memories of her mother's torture and abuse were some of the saddest recollections she ever made. Her new memories made it seem like her parents involved her in organized crime all of her life. Over many years, they showed her all the inner workings of the child pornography ring.

Soon she identified teachers she had while growing up who worked in the ring. At one point, she realized the club soccer organization, which she played for as a kid, covered up organized crime. The trips they took for soccer games served as covers for her parents' involvement in child trafficking.

At the same time, this child trafficking division began going through all the documents provided by Nicolas/Owen and all of the details Emma told them. They started uncovering all kinds of mind-boggling and complex aspects behind the operation.

The FBI found addresses of crime figures, jets, houses used for child brothels, even children. One afternoon at two, the FBI planned to raid one of the brothels. The phone rang, and Emma put Agent Johnson on speakerphone.

When Agent Johnson yelled, "MOVE," we sat scared on the edge of our seats waiting. Soon the reports came flooding back of all the kids they found. We loved those days.

Emma's agitation and anxiety grew. The agents who watched us left prescribed medication for Emma to take to sleep. This medication came in liquid form, and they put it in Gatorade. When she drank the medicated Gatorade, she typically relaxed and slept for a little while. It made her silly, and sometimes she reverted to a childlike state when she took it.

I never really understood this, but I understood the effects because I stayed up all night long with a wayward six-

or seven-year-old. With some memories, Emma passed out on the floor. She incessantly woke up inside memories shuddering. She bellowed and thrashed around for hours, all the while I said her name. I must have called her name painstakingly a million times.

I tried so hard to comfort her and prayed so hard for her to find peace and sleep. I barely saw clearly out of my own eyes. At times I felt so insignificant and isolated. I cried for her pains and then cried for mine. I comforted her then desperately needed comforting. I just wanted to sleep, to turn over in my own bed and not be needed every second of every day. I needed balance, distance, and time to cry. I wished to be rescued.

In the beginning I used my mind so much to try to reason my way through it all, but during this time, I quit trying. I pictured myself getting dragged behind a horse. I tried to describe how I felt to my husband, but words and pictures no longer described my pain.

During some of these later episodes, late at night, Agent Johnson texted me. We have found out how she did a lot of what she did, but some things we still do not know and probably never will.

By the end days, Agent Johnson texted me hundreds of times a day. He either had questions for her, or he updated me on what they found. He seemed to care about Emma like a daughter. Johnson had a dry sense of humor and a huge passion for saving children. When he began having to watch the torture videos, he started speaking to me about the ugliness of child trafficking and how sad all this made him. I felt terrible for him.

So many of her repressed memories were now unlocked.

Through evidence and her memories, the big picture of her life began to take shape, and so many missing pieces were unearthed. She had more and more long lost children. They used Emma like a baby-making factory to try to get more baby girls in the organization. Emma and Owen/Nicolas had a considerable history together in the ring. Owen, Jane, and the other kids they found to be hers also re-located somewhere about an hour from here.

Agent Johnson continued to arrange the visits, and she got to see them every couple of weeks. They showed us new pictures of Owen and the kids daily. Seeing them helped us to focus momentarily on good instead of evil.

The FBI asked Mike and me to adopt one of the little girls they rescued. After her rescue, the FBI sent us pictures of Riley on a United States jet. We agreed to adopt her. Riley had blond hair and blue eyes. Johnson sent us pictures of Riley almost every day. One of the higher up crime figures had custody of Riley, and when he went to jail, she needed a home. Agent Johnson told us after they eliminated parental rights, the adoption papers could be final. My husband and I had a picture of her on our phones and looked forward to meeting her.

We didn't question how the FBI handled itself. We understood why this group of men needed to be discreet; they had to see the most tragic things in their profession and had to infiltrate these porn rings. My husband and I felt honored by their service and decided to try to minister to them if possible.

We thought we heard Agent Johnson's voice on speakerphone; yet, we are still not sure whose voice we really heard. Maybe rules seemed to be broken, but at this point, this case developed into such a groundbreaking, gruesome, and unconventional one. It seemed everyone held on minute by minute, including the FBI.

A HIT MAN? ARE YOU KIDDING ME?

I wanted out. At times we didn't even trust the FBI. Due to our intense fear, we did not tell anyone or ask questions of anybody. Everywhere we walked, we looked over our shoulders. We often saw men following us. Once Emma got freaked out and ran out to the front of our house. We stood out front, trying to get her to come back inside, and within minutes, two men wearing black hoodies walked right by us.

We thought the FBI seriously planned to arrest us, or someone in organized crime might want to kill us. We didn't even talk freely to one another because, based on what we saw and heard, their top-notch surveillance picked up everything. I simply used the restroom or walked upstairs, and I received a text verifying my whereabouts and safety.

You would think this constant shadowing ought to make us feel safer. Initially it did, but ultimately it did not because we figured if they were watching us this closely, we must really be in danger. We always feared maybe they chose not to tell us something.

CRAZY IS AS CRAZY DOES

Much of my life continued out of control. I felt it, and I knew it, but I didn't know what to do. Brian rarely texted me. Ralph stayed busy with his own family problems. Due to the constant texting and calamity all around us, my efforts to accomplish anything at work became futile. Soon, another girl at work quit. Emma had worked busily behind the scenes to eliminate her.

Later we found out the lengths she had gone to and the lies she had told to ensure this girl's exit. Emma did not stop there. One more girl resigned before Emma's whole farce came out. Emma did enough of her job to get by and made it appear how hard she tried to heal and perform her work duties.

The morale fell in our office. It felt like a beloved friend you worked with had lost a battle with cancer or something. We didn't go to work all happy and excited any more. We went to work fighting and feeling sad. My thoughts continued to blur.

I can remember talking to my senior pastor, Jake, in a meeting and getting texts from Agent Johnson the whole time. He said something to me, and then my phone responded and told me what to say back to him. He stared at me so strangely like he thought I might be crazy.

Right toward the end of her evil schemes, I got the FBI to add Jake to the list of approved people. This made it possible for me to explain to Jake why so many of the girls quit. The FBI wanted Emma protected and felt adding him now may help her to stay safe. Emma did not make this easy: My own father and daughter did not make the list. My son made it on the list because he sometimes slept in our home, and I believe Emma wanted his sympathy.

According to what the FBI supposedly told us, they sent men to our church services, followed all of us, bugged all of the offices, and did background checks on all of our staff to keep everyone safe. Considering this whole thing unfolded in his church, with his staff, I just did not feel right about

Jake not knowing the specifics. Girls quit right and left, spirits dropped, and everyone in our office acted so differently. I felt like I needed to be able to tell him something about what was happening, if only for professional reasons.

Agent Johnson texted Jake, identified himself, and asked him to meet with me. Jake met with me, but when he did, our meeting quickly got cut short. I played out what words I should use. I planned to say, "Emma has been going through a very difficult time." I might say, "I know I have acted crazy lately, here's the reason why" or just, "HELP ME!"

We sat down at a large round table outside, and just then Agent Johnson texted me and told me he turned off the bugs so I could talk freely. I did not believe him and did not feel as if I could talk freely. However, I tried to at least give Jake some of the facts of the case. He sat down at the table very angry. I did not know why.

He did not appreciate receiving a text telling him to meet me by some stranger proclaiming to be an FBI agent. Besides, he had a board meeting he needed to prepare for, and he did not welcome this interruption. I talked fast, and as soon he heard about the bugs and the FBI's tactics in his church, he immediately put his guard up. The conversation pretty much ended. He demanded to meet Agent Johnson personally.

The option of meeting Agent Johnson did not exist. He threatened to call the police, which petrified all of us because we thought some of the local police might have been involved in this crime ring. To keep Jake quiet, Emma ended up meeting with Jake face-to-face. Jake and his wife, Allie, met with Emma, and she told them the complete story. I did not attend that meeting.

Jake and Allie sobbed for hours upon hearing her horrific

tale. They could not even fathom all of the atrociousness she shared. Afterward, they offered their support and encouragement to her. They checked in on her and prayed for her as well. I did not speak much to Jake about this; my concern focused more on Emma's safety and support. She told them all about the FBI, and they too honored the FBI's wishes and said nothing in order to protect her.

A few weeks later, we were told that Emma's parents went into custody. Then out of nowhere, Jake saw Emma's parents at a restaurant. He suspected something didn't make sense. Jake immediately questioned Emma on this, but she always had a convincing story as to why something seemed off. Agent Johnson texted a long message explaining the deal they made with her parents.

They told us not to approach them under any circumstances and assured us of our safety. Agent Johnson told us they intended to use Emma's parents to draw out others who might be deeply involved in this child pornography operation. We understood the importance of catching the bigger fish. We also knew if Emma had any chance of a safe and bright future, everyone involved must be taken down, and we must all be silent in the meantime.

THE LAST THIRTY DAYS

I remember one night when I was upstairs in my bedroom, I received a text from Agent Johnson. He sent me a picture of Emma in a ball on the floor behind one of my chairs. He came into my house and unsuccessfully tried to get her out of a particular memory for over an hour. He asked me to come downstairs, use my voice, and help to get her out of this tough memory.

I found her under a blanket crying behind my chair, her eyes closed, body shaking, and in a trance-like state. From that day until it ended, she slept in my bed next to me. Initially, my husband thought I might get more rest if she slept near me.

The last thirty days were the worst of any of the days up until then. Emma slept in my bed in perpetual, unspeakable, and horrendous memories. She screamed and cried, over and over, like a woman begging for someone to save her life. She told me that Reese forced her as a child to watch him murder other children and get her to participate. In these memories of when she was seven, she lit children on fire, drank their blood, took their skin off, and even buried them alive. Yes, she lived all those and more memories out while I documented them. During the last thirty days, I began having extreme anxiety.

I had no escape at this point. Unable to handle what I heard, I shut down. I went into my closet, sat down in front of the door, and cried. I tried to hide in there, and I desperately tried to get my thoughts together. It did not work. I needed to talk to someone about the images stuck in my mind and the negative thoughts and fears I had.

I stopped sleeping, and my irrational thoughts were surpassed by my rational brain. I have had past trauma in my life, and this case touched every one of my past triggers. I lost hope and the ability to cope. I suffered unremittingly.

The FBI assigned me a therapist. He spoke to me every day and got me out of the closet on many occasions. When I ended up in therapy after this terrible event was over, my real therapist said he used actual therapy techniques. Tears still come to my eyes when I rewind those desperate moments in the closet. Yet, I don't feel blameworthy anymore. The images tormented me to the point of physical anguish, and I know the depth of the agony that overtook me.

I felt a demonic presence often. I thought by helping Emma bring down a child pornography ring, the enemy unquestionably had reason to come against me. I rebuked him often! I played worship music every night, all night. In my distress, I prayed and cried out to God.

I struggled to hold on to myself, and I tried to hold on to God. When we were told that children escaped unharmed, we praised him! I believe Emma read my journals and used every letter God ever gave to me to help craft her conspiracy and make it appear like God moved throughout her story and our life with her. I always brought Emma's conversations back to God. She constantly felt ashamed and devastated.

"Tracy, how will I ever have any kind of life now?"

"Emma, God knows you and sees you and cares deeply for you. I know it doesn't feel like it, but the revelations you are having now will be used to heal you."

"Do you think it's my fault this happened to me?" she asked.

"No! Emma, God hates what your father did to you. He hates what all those other men did to you. He will give you a new life, I promise."

Throughout this story, we used the term pinky promise to signify we meant our words. So many lies lived in Emma's past, and so many people abused her trust, we promised to stay by her side. So if she felt unsure about us or our dedication to her, she would say, "Pinky promise?"

And we would respond, "Pinky promise!" Emma and her

brothers used pinky promise all while growing up.

After she began to digest the reality of her memories, she often would say to my husband and me, "I have no family."

We often replied, "We will be your new family; you will never be alone."

She always looked firmly at us and said, "Pinky promise?"

To show her our devotion, we all went one night and got tattoos on our pinky fingers. The tattoo reads "promise." We wanted her to feel loved. The FBI texted us to let us know every single one of the agents got the tattoo also. Kara, Bailey, and my son Adam got the tattoo as well.

I used every opportunity given to teach and example the love of God to this broken girl. I wanted her to feel new and worth something. I spoke truth, light, and encouragement over everyone involved every day.

Have you ever given someone the best of you, and in return, felt betrayed, used, and even victimized by their very hand? For some of us, this person might be a spouse, child, friend, boss, co-worker, or even a family member. The sudden pain and isolation we feel when we have set out to do right and the wrong thing comes can tear us apart and suffocate us.

Confusion quickly beckons, and if you're like me, tears join the party. The "why" questions keep playing like a song stuck in your head, and the wishing it never happened settles in deep.

I gave Emma the best of God and the best of me. In return, Emma sought to devour me.[1]

FIVE

EASTER BOMBSHELL

I washed my clothes and loaded my car with the things I needed for the next few hours. I wasn't quite sure how all the services would play out or if I would even be able to get in to see one of them. I soon arrived at the church, and, in what seemed like seconds, eight jam-packed holiday services got underway.

All of a sudden, people needed to know where to go, and I heard sounds of snack carts flying by me. I tried to think about Easter and everything it meant, but my brain only went to one place—Emma and the story I now knew about her. I struggled to conceive of such malice happening to an innocent young child, let alone Emma. I reeled in constant disarray, mourning the loss of innocence, purity, wonder, and kindness in the world.

My eyes hurt, and my body felt exhausted from days of no sleep. My tears lived right at the surface of my eyes, just waiting to pour out. I missed my family and friends, and I did not know which direction led to the life I used to have. The life I used to love was hidden behind a mountain of pain.

Easter has always been a time of restoration and renewal for my family. I have started companies, moved jobs, and took on new projects all around Easter. When all of Emma's lies got exposed on Easter Sunday, I did not say,

"Wow, how renewing!" I said, "This is the worst nightmare and the saddest day ever!" Funny now to think about how God, in all his power, allowed the truth to come out on Easter. Jesus is our living hope and brought hope that day. He broke the power of sin and darkness once again smack dab in the middle of my living room.

Honestly, this Easter proved to be the most powerful breakthrough of renewal in my life so far; I just didn't see it that day. A nightmare ended on Easter, and at the same time, a new one began.

Easter Sunday ranks up there as a pretty big day for pastors with lots of church services, new faces, and work to do. I can remember running around frantic, trying to land a few planes, making sure the programing for all the kids stayed in place, and trying to keep my head above water. I had not slept longer than a couple of hours in over a month. There's a great lesson on balance.

I knew I landed in a bad place. I felt miserable and alone on an island. Trying to survive, I clung to my fake therapist. I had stopped eating, and my thoughts and feelings made no sense. I did make plans to get time alone or sleep for a bit and something, that something being Emma always had an emergency I had to tend to. When services ended, we decided to go home. Emma planned with Agent Johnson to see her kids on Easter.

We had shopped for their Easter baskets, and I felt excited for Emma to give their baskets to them. I looked forward to Emma, Owen, and the kids spending time together on Easter. Owen continued to email me often, and with each email, his anticipation grew and grew. I planned to rest and see my husband for a couple of hours.

My husband and I hadn't had a second alone in more than thirty days. After we got home, Emma received a text within minutes. The FBI picked her up in a black car with very dark windows. She got into this car, and it took her to the location of the kids. I did see one of these cars. I couldn't wait for her to leave. I needed a minute to myself. She walked out the door and, three minutes later, my husband said, "I need to talk to you." Then he followed with, "Do you promise not to pick up your phone while we talk?"

"Yes...why, what's going on?"

"You must let me finish."

Feeling a little nervous, I said, "Okay..." Concern washed over my face, but I complied.

"I planted cameras all over our house, put string on all of our windows, and installed a tracking device in Emma's car."

Instantly scared, I said, "WHAT?" I did not want us to get into trouble, and I felt he risked our safety.

"I have been staying up every night, staking out the FBI houses." He had dressed in all black, left his phone by the bed, and snuck out of our house. I can still see him in my mind crawling through the grass. The FBI used two houses, one for work and one where the men slept. He staked out the big house where they worked. We commonly saw ten to twenty cars in front of this house at all times. He wrote down all the license plates of the ones coming and going to that house. He hid in the bushes and laid on the ground, so no cars, people, or FBI saw him.

"Are you crazy?"

"No one is coming into our house." He said, "The strings I put on the doors and windows at night stayed intact." Again he repeated, "The FBI is not coming in our house!"

"What are you saying right now? This can't be possible!"

"The cameras showed nothing and nobody, Tracy."

The FBI allegedly had come into our house every night for the last month. No way he could be correct; someone came into our house. One time there were items on the island for them, and my text said to stay upstairs. When I came downstairs, they were gone.

One night after a long conversation and strenuous therapy for Emma, we told the FBI we would set a trap for them. If they got through the trap, fun treats would be waiting for them on our kitchen island. (We had played games with them sometimes.)

Agent Johnson laughed and had said, "Bring it on."

So we tied yarn everywhere like a game of cat's cradle and tied bells to the yarn.

Later that evening and late into the night while Emma slept on the couch, our front door opened and a flashlight shined in and looked around a bit, and then the door shut. The next day, they told us they had come by to get the stuff, but with lots of bail hearings the next morning, they didn't have time to play the game, but they wanted to at least check in on us.

Every word out of my husband's mouth stunned me. Then Mike said, "Emma is not with her kids today."

"What do you mean?"

He showed me his phone, which revealed the camera he had planted in her car. It revealed that the car was parked at her parents' house. Processing this information at that moment proved to be impossible.

Emma's parents previously went to jail, but we still thought the FBI needed them as bait to draw out those deeper inside the organization. Emma's parents stayed under complete surveillance. Emma remained very estranged from her parents. So for her to be at her parents' house seemed absolutely outlandish—not only outlandish but impossible because of the danger they posed to her.

"Tracy, she went home for Easter!" I couldn't breathe.

He said, "Look." I looked at the phone and sure enough, the feed I watched showed Emma walking into her parents' house.

"Why would she be there?"

Then he showed me the pictures he had taken of inside her trunk the day prior. "I snuck her keys away from her yesterday and searched her car." My husband is Jason Bourne.

As he scrolled through his pictures, I saw all kinds of things that did not belong in her car. Gifts for her fake kids, books, Bibles, journals, and all kinds of things that I thought had gone over to the FBI house filled her trunk. About a week before, we had made two huge pans of enchiladas from scratch and sent them over to the FBI house for the agents. Those same two pans of enchiladas were hidden in her trunk.

I looked at him and said, "What do you mean the enchiladas are in her trunk? Agent Johnson said they loved them."

"No, Tracy, the enchiladas never went to the FBI." Slowly he began again, "Tracy, the enchiladas you made from scratch are in her trunk."

As he started rambling all of these things out, I thought he had lost his mind. I looked at the proof, which showed his mind to be the only mind thinking clearly.

"What made you look in her trunk?"

"I already knew no one visited us at night, and I couldn't

shake the awful feeling in my stomach. I had so many new questions and needed answers." He missed me very much and had a tough time adjusting to not talking and sleeping in the same bed at night.

He sprayed my perfume on his pillow just to get some sleep. He came in each night to tuck me in before he went to bed and each morning to say goodbye before he left for work, but that's it. We didn't text much because we knew we had no privacy. At this point, Mike had lost over 20 pounds. He struggled with thoughts of sadness and saw the life he cherished disappearing. He also saw the toll this had taken on me. He had no confidence that this nightmare would end any time soon and that worried him. He wanted his wife back. Thank God!

He would tell you that, in his eyes, I went missing. In my eyes, I got lost. I didn't wake him up much in the night anymore because I knew he needed his rest. He had to be up early and had to perform physical work during the day. As the days turned into months and the stories became more shocking and despicable, he just wanted it all to end. We both did.

"When did this start?"

"One night I felt desperate, I laid in bed awake and began to pray like I have never prayed before, and I clearly heard from God. I wrote what God said to me in this journal." He showed me the journal. (He even had to look some of the words up because they were in other languages.)

"Then what?"

"Then I did every step God told me to do."

I still wrestle with this on some days. I think, *Why didn't*

God tell me? Why didn't he show me the truth? Here I did everything for the right reason, with the right heart, and God didn't speak to me? Why?

"Tracy, I drank her medication."

"WHAT, YOU DID WHAT?"

"Well, about a week ago... remember when we got home from going to church in L.A.?"

"Yes."

"A new Gatorade bottle with her medication sat on the nightstand next to your bed." This bottle did not sit on the counter when we left. Agent Johnson texted me and told me they put it there. "I got home before Emma, and I saw it and switched it out for regular Gatorade. Then I went downstairs with the medication and drank it! Nothing happened to me so then I came back upstairs and watched her drink her fake medication."

"What happened?"

"I watched her pretend to fall asleep in seconds."

"Why didn't you say anything to me?" I was distraught by this time..

"I could not be sure what was really going on. I knew the medication was fake, but I did not know if the FBI was real. At the time, I needed to try to figure out the truth and why all of this was happening. I needed to find out if she was lying or the FBI was lying. I was unsure of what to do next. So I kept praying."

"Then what?"

"You're not going to like this."

"I don't like any of this already."

Then he said, "I asked Adam to help me."

I was so upset, "Adam? You brought Adam into this?"

"I couldn't trust anyone else."

He had enlisted the help of our son Adam to help him get to the bottom of things. My son lived about thirty minutes away, so he witnessed none of this. I stopped sharing details with him some time ago when it got so wretched. After Mike called him, my son later told me he began praying non-stop, and one night when he prayed, a bottle in his room shattered. I believe dark forces were at work.

My husband and son were petrified to tell anyone but did it anyway. My son knew a police officer, and they decided to meet covertly and seek counsel from him. They gave him the license plate numbers of all the cars in the driveways of the FBI houses. This policeman guided them and told them what to do next. We later found out that all the cars lined up there every day belonged to the owner of the home. He owned a used car lot.

RACE TO UNDERSTAND

Deception is one of Satan's most valued tools. I think most of us have experienced some level of deception in our lives, some more than others. Those of us who have been deeply deceived know the drill. The race to understand, dissect the truth, and make sense of the repercussions can be debilitating. Our minds are powerful; when we are truly misled, we instantly become like little search engines.

Flashback after flashback started taking over my conscious mind. The *why* questions toppled the *how* questions, and both formed quickly into incomplete sentences. Shock took over, and fear set in.

When we feel desperate, disillusioned, and full of despair, we begin to question everything and everyone. Those

unanswered questions, partnered with the unavoidable consequences of getting the answers to these same questions,
can lead us to a chaotic and deserted place.

SIX

ESCAPED BUT NOT YET FREE

Seconds after he told me all of this and before I had a chance to even respond to my husband, my phone started blowing up with texts from Agent Johnson.

I looked at Mike and said, "Can I answer the texts now?"

"Yes."

Easter morning Agent Johnson asked us not to go by her parents' house because his team planned some sort of sting there.

"Why is your son here?" the text read. "We asked you not to come here."

I quickly responded, "I had no idea my son went over there!" My husband then told me how Adam followed Emma. When Emma walked into her parents' house for Easter, she saw my son.

Then Emma texted, "I can't do this anymore."

"Why not?" I replied.

"They made me go to my parents' house. They said it wouldn't look right if I wasn't there. I got in the car, thinking I was going to see Owen and the kids, and they drove to my parents. I hate my parents!"

"Come home, and we can work everything out." On the one hand, I needed her to come home; I needed to find out the truth. At the same time, I felt scared. I kept thinking the old enchiladas are in her car. Who keeps enchiladas in their trunk for weeks? Suddenly I transported myself inside a creepy, scary movie in my mind. As much as Mike uncovered, we still really had no idea of Emma's end game.

We knew she lied. We knew people did not come into our home at night. We knew she went to her parents. We knew none of our food or gifts went to the FBI or her children. We did not know why. We did not know where reality ended and falsehood began.

Emma left her parents' house abruptly, drove to Target, and sat in the parking lot. We think she nervously went there to delete items off her phone. She finally came home, as did my son, and we confronted her first about the items in her trunk.

I said, "Emma, look we have given over four months to you, and this case and things are not adding up."

"What do you mean?" she asked.

I continued, "Mike put cameras everywhere and searched your trunk, and he found all the things that I thought you took to the FBI."

She looked up to the ceiling at the air vent and said, "Johnson texted me and told me they couldn't accept gifts from us, not even food."

"Why wouldn't Johnson tell us that?" I replied.

"I don't know," she started jabbering. "They said they didn't want to hurt your feelings so they asked me to move the items."

We didn't know what to believe because her story seemed plausible as usual. Then I wondered if she really ever got ahold of the real FBI. Maybe danger surrounded us. From there, I just kept asking more and more questions.

I needed something tangible. I thought back to all the texts from Johnson as he read the books we sent. His words, "We loved the enchiladas" flashed back to me. I kept thinking about the stories she told me of how her daughter Jane loved the pajamas I gave her and did not want to take them off, or how she played with the stuffed animals I sent. Those pajamas and those stuffed animals sat clear as day in her trunk. It did not make sense. After seeing all that stuff in her trunk, I couldn't trust her. I then asked her to call her brother Brian. "Emma, I need you to call Brian."

"Why, I'm not lying to you?"

"Well, I want to believe you, Emma, but right now after seeing all the stuff in your trunk, I'm concerned."

"He is at my parents, and the FBI is there."

"So."

"Well, I just left there all mad, and he can't talk in front of them."

"He can go outside."

I desperately wanted to talk to Brian because I knew him, I had met him, and I needed him to tell me this whole thing was not a lie. I wanted her to call him from her phone.

After her initial push back, she eventually dialed his number. He answered, and on speaker, I asked him a few questions about the case only he knew the answer to.

"Brian?" He hesitated like he had people around him and couldn't speak freely. After much hesitation, he answered all of my questions correctly.

"Brian, I need to know what's going on."

"Okay."

"I am here with Emma, and I want to ask you a couple of questions."

"Okay."

"Did you give Agent Johnson an IV when he got very sick?"

"...Yes."

"Did you sew up the little boy's throat—the one the FBI rescued on a raid?"

"...Yes."

"Did you help me with my medical problems?"

"...Yes."

The way he delayed answering concerned me. I wasn't satisfied. I asked Emma to show me the number she dialed, which she did. Then I asked her to show me the contact number on her text screen when she texts Brian—she mostly texts him all day long. She got very panicky and slid her finger all over her phone, saying, "It's the same... It's the same!"

Then she began reading off numbers. When she read off the numbers really fast, trying to prove her case, she didn't realize my husband wrote them down. The numbers did not match. The number she dialed was not the number she texts to. Then after a while, things stopped going anywhere, and my son got angry.

Adam yelled, "Emma, we want to believe you, but you need to be honest about what's going on!"

She continued to talk nonsense. "I showed you the numbers, they are the same... I can't do this anymore."

In a flat-out direct tone, Adam said, "Fine, if you're not going to tell us what's going on, we're calling your brother ourselves!" Then he read the number my husband had written down out loud. She recognized that number, that's for sure. He punched the number in his phone and pushed send. Emma freaked out! She came running over, trying to grab the phone out of my son's hand, getting physical with him, yelling, and carrying on.

"STOP... STOP...STOP..." she screamed.

He got away from her and ran out front. The phone began to ring, and sure enough, Brian answered—the real Brian. Adam began asking him questions about the FBI, abuse, repressed memories, and so on. Brian said he had no knowledge about any of that. Brian said, "I'll be right over, what is your address?"

Adam gave him our address. He sounded confused, stunned, and in shock. Within minutes he knocked at our front door. In those minutes, my mind jumped around and around. If Brian did not know anything, then who texted me thousands of times? Why did he lie? My attention turned to Emma.

"Emma, what is going on?" I demanded.

Knowing Brian had just left for our house, she had to think fast.

Finally she blurted out, "I didn't want to tell my brothers because I knew how upsetting it would be to them."

"What do you mean you didn't tell your brothers?" My mind started working overtime and suddenly, puzzle pieces began to fall into place.

"I knew they would freak out. I just couldn't tell them."

"What about Ralph—he doesn't know?" I started rambling, "Wait—he was close friends with law enforcement; he was the one you turned in the evidence to?" And then I thought: *If that's the case, where did the evidence go?*

"Ralph doesn't know," Emma replied.

"What about the FBI, Emma... What about the FBI, Emma?" She started crying, and hesitantly, I asked, "Who is

Johnson? You will tell me right this second who Johnson is, or I will call 911!" I grabbed my phone, ready to dial.

She then said the fateful words, "There is no FBI."

"Who were we talking to all these months, and who is Agent Johnson?"

"Me. I am Johnson."

SATAN HATES ME

If I didn't know it before, I know it now, Satan hates me. Satan's schemes were laid, plans were formed to bring me to ruin and destruction, and through God's grace, I escaped what he intended to use to hurt me.

We have escaped like a bird from the fowler's snare; the snare has been broken, and we have escaped. Our help is in the name of the Lord, the Maker of heaven and earth (Psalm 124:7 NIV).

Satan, and wicked men under his influence, are like fowlers who lay snares for them, to draw them into sin, into immorality and error, in order to bring them to ruin and destruction; hence we read of the snare of the devil and of wicked men, 1 Timothy 3:7, 2 Timothy 2:26; and who form plans and lay schemes to oppress and destroy them; but through the wisdom given them to discern these devices and stratagems, and through the power of divine grace, accompanying them, they escape what was intended for their hurt, and particularly in the following manner:

The snare is broken, and we are escaped; measures concerted by wicked men are broken, their schemes are confounded, their devices are disappointed, so that they cannot perform their enterprise; and by this means the saints escape the evils designed against them, the afflictions of the world, and the temptations of Satan *(Gill's Exposition of the Entire Bible).*

ESCAPED BUT NOT FREE

Seconds after the words came out of Emma's mouth, I cried out to the Lord, grief-stricken and overwhelmed. While mourning over my sorrowful state, the never-ending questions commenced:

Where is the money that we gave to her and her fake children?

Who was my fake therapist?

How did she do this?

Where did it begin?

How did she know the things she did?

How did I miss this?

What about the bloody nose?

What about all the letters I got from Owen?

Was God not talking to me?

Was I not discerning?

Who shined a flashlight in my house?

How did I become so isolated?

Who was texting me when she was asleep?

Is her fiancé involved?

Are there bugs in my house?

How was this person able to infiltrate my entire life, hijacking my notes, journals, and emails?

Are there cameras in my house?

How could a person move into my home and prey upon kindness?

Am I safe?

Were there no kids rescued?

How could a person manufacture every disturbing detail after detail?

Is she possessed?

Who else is involved?

She didn't do this alone!

So the stories about the agent's families were a lie?

Will I ever be the same?

Does she have a split personality?

Will I ever trust anyone ever again?

Who am I?

Why?

What now?

As traumatized and distraught as we felt that Easter evening, my husband and I went to Jake and Allie's house right away to tell them the truth. I did not want one person to spend one more night believing Emma's lies. I remember getting there and telling them Emma lied. I remember Jake looking at me and asking, "Are you okay, or are you just tired?"

I can remember saying, "I'm so tired." I don't remember driving home from their house.

Mike seemed to take the news easier than I did, I think because he knew for weeks of her capability for lying. Knowing that Emma pretended to be Agent Johnson brought me excruciating pain, while it brought Mike peace and satisfaction.

The next morning and although the sun came through the windows, the darkness lay heavy upon me. I did not know what to do first. So after a few hours of madness in my mind, my son said, "We need to get rid of everything in this house that has any association with Emma." I agreed.

With the help of friends and family, we threw every single thing that reminded us of Emma in the trash. Whenever something fell into the large, dark circular trashcan, I felt more and more rid of her. When we picked up each item, we hashed over the memory of the item and the entire story that attached itself to it—the blanket that covered her during her memories, the blue Gatorade in the fridge, the coffee cup she drank from, and the gifts she had given us all slammed into the trash.

The following day, I returned all the gifts we found in her trunk, the same gifts we bought in love for all the fake people. I missed one week of work. I cried until scabs formed under my eyes. I can remember going into one of the stores and accidently catching my reflection in the mirror on the wall. I had to take a second look because I did not recognize myself. I looked at my son and said, "Adam, why did you let me go out of the house looking like this?"

"Mom, you look great," he replied. I did not look great. I looked scary.

I felt like I needed glasses to see the world, and someone just stole them. I made my way through the dark maze feeling as I went. Mike and Adam took shifts with me. I can gladly say I did not physically go into the closet during this time. I did, however, go into therapy.

About a week after the truth came barreling through our lives, Mike and I met with Emma's parents and her brother Ralph. Emma's family did not want to hear the details of what happened. They expressed their concern for their daughter and their apologies on her behalf. As hurtful as this felt, we had to realize that our pain didn't translate into their pain.

I spoke to the police multiple times. She never stole anything, except months of our lives. She didn't commit a crime punishable by law. Ralph let us know they took her to a psychiatric hospital to be evaluated. The chief of police told us once someone gets diagnosed with a mental disorder, the DA assumes it would be an insanity case, which they would lose. So chances are they wouldn't take the case, unless there were real damages.

We did not want a thing from her—especially money. We did not want to spend one more minute going over any of the specifics of this story with anyone. We wanted Emma and her lunacy to go away and stay away. We did not wish pain for her family and truly wanted her to get help.

After we did all of the obvious things like getting her keys back, finalizing her removal from ministry, and changing all of our passcodes, no obvious path for me emerged.

I forgot what normal felt like. My painful crying and sobbing filled the air, and I began to wake up numb and disoriented. Grief-stricken and overwhelmed, I cried out to the

Lord. I gave myself great big pep talks. I walked around the block talking to God until I couldn't walk another step. I sat for hours, reasoning about it all.

I kept thinking, *I am a children's pastor who has dedicated my existence to love and serve kids, and I fight wholeheartedly against injustice, so how is this happening to me?* I didn't understand how such demonic influence got in my own home. Did God leave me? I know demons did not possess me. I know they oppressed me. Nevertheless, I pray against Satan; I don't watch bad stuff; I do not invite evil in my home or my life. I keep the doors to anything demonic slammed shut. So how did this direct assault of the enemy take shape?

I found myself, without a doubt, lost in a sea of betrayal and swimming in an ocean of bewilderment. I couldn't see through the trees. I had to cry; I had to walk through days of numbness to even find my toothbrush. I sat emotionally and physically sickened, fully grieving, and in between sobs, wondered how this happened. *How will I ever recover?* Being so disconnected, out of balance, and blindsided left me totally unsure of myself and my future.

Let me take a break and tell you that I know all the Christian explanations. Rain will fall on the just and the unjust[2]. There is sin in the world, and bad things happen. As a pastor, I know first-hand how bad things happen to good people. Missionaries are taken hostage, kids are molested, and wonderful godly people die of horrible, ungodly diseases. Bad things have happened to me, and I got through them with a greater understanding of God. This time felt different.

Have you ever felt so far away from home and been so

lost in a forest of fear and shock that all you could do was search for something, anything to guide you—a treetop, some footprints, a little brook, a landmark of any kind.

When you're lost, you look for landmarks. You look for something familiar to ease your spirit and guide you. You watch the skies and the sun for signs. You cry out for someone to hear you. HELP! I'M LOST! CAN ANYONE HEAR ME?

I felt so small in the scheme of things, like a little girl in a big forest lost with the sun going down. I frantically went looking for landmarks to guide me home to safety. And I prayed with all I had that God could hear me.

SEVEN

THROUGH THE FLAMES

My favorite movie scenes are the ones when a 9.9 earthquake or the strongest hurricane known to man has just hit. Explosions occur, and debris flies everywhere. No human being could have ever survived this disaster. Then, sure enough, an action hero like Matt Damon, Scarlett Johansson, or Mark Wahlberg runs straight through the fire.

They left destruction and desolation behind them as they emerged in one piece, usually covered in black marks, have bloodstained clothes, and sometimes are limping. The crowd cheers, relief builds, and gratification fills everybody in the audience. Everyone watched secretly on the edge of his or her seat, hoping for a victorious ending.

Often when an actor comes through such devastation, he comes out different, doesn't he? He seems ready to conquer the world in a whole new way; you can see grit, determination, and conquest all over his face. They usually don't show us the redemption scene, but deep down, we all know he is going straight from the survival scene full of burning flames to get the girl, win his family back, or make wrongs right. As the music plays and credits begin to travel up the screen, we go home elated because we saw someone overcome what seemed like insurmountable challenges; we saw good triumph over evil.

WHAT'S YOUR FIRE?

Some of us may see ourselves coming through the fire after a 5K. We see ourselves shouting, "I did it!" For others, it may be winning a battle with cancer, getting a big promotion, or accomplishing something huge on a bucket list.

When something traumatic or extremely sad happens in my life, I easily picture myself in the wreckage. Tears and fears are on rewind without trying. Yet, there are a few very distinct times in my life where I can replay a scene and see myself so clearly and gloriously running out of the fire, not looking back.

It's these same conquering scenes that keep me confident and hopeful. When I am in the middle of a 9.9 earthquake in my life, I can honestly say to myself, remember when you made it through that last hurricane?

DO YOU HAVE A REDEMPTION SCENE IN YOUR MOVIE?

As you have seen, trauma the size of a natural disaster crashed unexpectedly in my life and threatened to take out everything in its path. Some say whistles blew, or sirens must have rung to warn me; however, I did not hear them if they did. When the severe destruction and damage hit, I wasn't ready. How do you get prepared for an unexpected death, mind-bending betrayal, or a horrific accident?

I am not sure how anyone gets prepared to give CPR to their dying mother, fish their dead son's body out of a swimming pool, or find out a person you cared for has ruthlessly deceived you. Unfortunately, those are some of the shocking truths I have had to wrestle with in the dark. I realized I could never have been truly ready for any of those things to hit my life, yet they did.

As shocked, lonely, scared, and destroyed as I have been in the past, with God's help, I have come through the fire over and over again. God's deliverance in the past reminds me of what I can endure with his great grace in the future. Our personal redemption stories have the power to turn us away from fear, doubt, and disbelief. Through the fire, I have gained faith, grown in strength, learned to trust him no matter what may happen, matured in him, been able to share wisdom with others, and found peace I thought was gone forever.

Just like the pillar Ebenezer stood as a monument set up by Samuel to remind Israel of God's strong hand and their triumph[3], we too can have epic moments, memories, and a rich redemptive history to remind us of God's victory in our lives. Has God ever led you out of the fire?

FROM WHERE DO OUR NIGHTMARES COME?

The summer after sixth grade, I flew alone to South Dakota for a six-week vacation. Instead of having a wonderful summer experience out of state while staying with long lost family, I suddenly became full of apprehension, fearfulness, and hopelessness. The people I stayed with mistreated me. When my mom or family called to check in on me, they picked up the other line and listened to every word of our conversations. They wanted to make sure I did not say a word about the abuse.

They glared at me while I talked on the phone with my parents, while at the same time motioning me with their hands to not say a word. They terrified me. I knew my family planned to come for me in six weeks, but this brought me no comfort as a child. I had no concept of time, so six weeks seemed like sixty years.

During this time, fear filled my days. I thought my parents might die, I may never see my family again, and more harm would come to me. I was in the fire.

At one point, I escaped without them knowing. I went frantically running down a long dirt road searching for help. I found a pay phone and, as fast as I could, began dialing my mom's work phone number. I used to call my mom after school at her work, so I knew the number. I still have nightmares of mistakenly punching in the numbers over and over again. Desperately, I pushed zero to get the operator. I shouted on the phone to the operator to help me. "Please, this call is collect!"

I was dying to hear my mom's voice. In what seemed like forever, the operator got through to a woman receptionist who finally accepted the collect call.

"Please, can I talk to Trudie Hicks?"

She said, "Just a moment, please" and began to transfer me. My heart pounded loud in my ears. I feverishly practiced everything I planned to say to my mom in my head. I wanted to be able to tell her quickly, "I am *not* okay," and "Come and rescue me!" My mom would have been there to pick me up in minutes if she had known.

She hoped for me to have the adventure of my life. My family counted down the days for me to experience this fun once-in-a-lifetime vacation in the midwest. I thought about how disappointed my family would be when they found out all their hopes and dreams for me didn't happen.

The people I stayed with must have quickly realized I left.

In a matter of minutes, they drove up and told me to get in the car, and within seconds I lost all hope. I hung up the phone, despondently got in the car, and never got to speak to my mom that day. They took me back to their house where I stayed for every second of what remained of those six weeks. I did not eat, I did not sleep, and I did not function normally. I still wonder what they thought would transpire when I eventually got to really talk to my family. Did they think their bullying ensured my silence forever? I am still not sure what they thought.

DO YOU HEAR GOD'S VOICE?

The house I stayed in had an old, white, rickety swing on the front porch. Each day I sat for hours or as long as they let me in that porch swing. In the beginning, I made my way to the swing and cried out to the Lord over and over to help me. I know some may say I was just a kid, but I believed in God. My grandma Myrt always read the Bible to me. When I became so distressed and had nowhere else to turn, I turned to God. One day after I finished crying, I heard my name, "Tracy."

I listened closely, and sure enough, I heard it again, "Tracy." There are not many ways to describe this other than God opened the floodgates of his grace to me. God spoke to me as clear as day. I did not know about worship music; I hadn't read fifty books on the subject; I hadn't heard multiple sermons on hearing from God. I didn't doubt myself, and I didn't doubt God. God spoke to me not in words but chapters. He reassured me and taught me how to get through every step of that horrific summer. He told me how to walk in and eat something. He told me where to sit and exactly what to say and when to say it.

He said things like, "Tracy, today is the day you will wash your hair." We had a month-long conversation, which never stopped. He was so funny; he made jokes to make me laugh. Yes, God is funny! I laughed so hard on that swing. I told him about every fear, deep dark secret, doubt, ache, and pain. He saw me, he saw my situation, he heard me, and he directly spoke to me. He helped me to focus on things to help me get home safe.

Soon I didn't need the swing to hear from him. I just talked to him all the time, non-stop. I asked him everything I thought of, and he answered me. I cried so much with him, and he comforted me. When I think back, it is still so surreal. When I remember the conversations, it seemed like I was talking to my friend in front of me. He answered swiftly and clearly.

Sometimes, I didn't always grasp what he told me, but he explained until I understood. I trusted him explicitly. As a child, I never really tried to figure any of this out. I just believed so purely and innocently.[4]

There is no figuring out the mysteries of God, but as you can imagine, as I got older, I sure tried. Over the years, Satan tried to steal this memory from me many times, whispering all kinds of questions and doubts in my mind. It can be very hard as adults to hear God's voice amidst our own uncertainties, desires, thoughts, life's distractions, and especially pain.

I believe hearing his voice at such a young age is one reason I can hear him so distinctly today. Looking back into my past and knowing without a shadow of a doubt that God spoke to me has given me an unrelenting hope in him. It gives me a redemption scene to hold on to when my feet begin to blister from the red-hot coals dropping around me, and the smoke begins to burn my eyes.

I can tell you when the spirit of doubt covers me like a shadow; I just take myself back to this time in my mind and begin talking to God again. Then in no time at all, I hear "Tracy," and he talks right back. Soon I can see myself running through the fire, hair blowing, free, safe, and not looking back!

Dr. Wess Stafford, president of Compassion International, states, "Childhood—we get only one pass at it, and yet it dictates the quality of the rest of our lives. What we think, feel, experience, and endure in this earliest phase is the single most important indicator of what the rest of life is going to be like." I agree with him.

Those weeks of such pain and despair served as my door out of pain and despair over and over again in my life. I guess we never know when we are in the midst of suffering how God will use it later to minister to others and us. I was lost, and he found me.[5] This hardship shaped me into who I am today and continually fuels my faith and passion for ministry?

Hardship often prepares an ordinary person for an extraordinary destiny. –C.S. Lewis

I became a children's pastor as a result of my time on the porch swing. I knew firsthand that teaching kids to hear from God while they are young gives them a landmark to return to that will help them to trust him in the future. They will recognize his voice, especially in situations that threaten to take them down and burn them up.[6]

IS THAT YOU, GOD?

When I heard Emma say, "There is no FBI" and "I made it all up," I felt like I went outside my body. Whatever blazes I went through in the past faded in comparison to this. Desperate for the porch swing, I saw myself gasping for air, running through an unknown neighborhood as ash and smoke surrounded me. Then I envisioned running from house to house searching for the porch swing, and at house after house, I found nothing.

I just wanted God to explain why this occurred. I needed to know how all of this absurdity happened to me. I wanted to hear his soft voice speak to me and say, "You are okay." I wanted to hear his fatherly advice begin outlining what I needed to do next. I longed to hear God shout in an audible voice, "You are safe, and this is not your fault!" I wanted to trust God with my whole heart and mind. I needed peace like I needed air. I knew God had never left me, yet the darkness closed in on me. I didn't see God, and I sure couldn't feel him.

I never felt more abandoned by God than after Emma's deceitfulness. I have experienced my fair share of trauma and pain in my life with my mother's sudden death, the drowning of my son, and even the summer in South Dakota. Out of all of my ordeals, this one presented the greatest trial. Why?

I decided if I could be so misled in trusting Emma and be so terribly mistaken, then I couldn't trust myself to discern anything, especially God's voice. The fact that this wickedness happened inside my ministry just left me more muddled. More than anything, I feared hearing God wrong. God still spoke to me, but I shut down and didn't trust what I heard.

I went through the motions for weeks. I walked, listened to worship music, got out my yellow paper and pencil and wrote down what I heard. As much as I wanted to believe I heard God like I used to, I just couldn't. I felt numb. Nothing breached my wall. I didn't trust myself, and sadly, I didn't know how to trust God with my life going forward. How do I trust a God who didn't protect me from this much pain?

Feelings of fear, loneliness, hopelessness, foolishness, confusion and sadness overcame me. I had no plans to give up on God or my beliefs, but I questioned his plan for me. I feared the future. I froze in a tremendous spirit of dread, wondering what awful thing might happen next. Fear steals the truth right from under us. It may be hard to draw a perfect picture for you; however, I will try.

I always believed in God's sovereignty, and I resigned myself long ago to the fact that he gets to decide what goes on in this world. It's almost like when I was a kid, and my dad said no more ice cream or else you will get sick. I wanted more ice cream, but I trusted my dad because he knew best. I believed in the power of prayer and never stopped praying. When all this happened, I just felt insignificant in the whole scheme of things.

For example, the day my mom died, I had begged and pleaded with God for her not to die. Then she died. I knew when she died, he had a plan. I didn't agree with his methods that day, but I understood he is God and I loved him, knew he loved me, and knew he loved her. I did not get angry or blame God in a bad way.

I realized his ways are not always our ways.[7] I just felt irrelevant and inconsequential, almost like his plans are great for him, but his plans hurt me. With the Emma nightmare, I saw God in control but not taking control of protecting me. I questioned whether he ignored my cries for help or lost track of me somehow. I wondered if I did something wrong. Why did it take so long for me to be delivered from her?

DESTROYING OUR TRUST IN GOD

I love how the Bible gives us permission to feel and ask hard questions. It doesn't take much time, paging through our Bibles, to find great men of God feeling lost, full of questions, in darkness, and isolated from God. I love how Jesus, Job, and David gave us their hearts on their sleeves. I appreciate their authenticity with God, with themselves, and with us.

Jesus cried out to God, and he too felt deserted by God, so I guess I joined good company. "About three in the afternoon Jesus cried out in a loud voice, "Eli, Eli, lama sabachthani?" (This means "My God, my God, why have you forsaken me?") in Matthew 27:46 (NIV). Job felt surrounded by darkness and abandoned.

That is why I am terrified before him; when I think of all this, I fear him. God has made my heart faint; the Almighty has terrified me. Yet I am not silenced by the darkness, by the thick darkness that covers my face (Job 23: 15-17 NIV).

Tragedies in David's life made him feel forsaken by God. "My God, my God, why have you forsaken me? Why are you so far from saving me, so far from my cries of anguish?" (Psalm 22:1 NIV)

Working in ministry allows me a rare glimpse into tragedy and people's suffering. I see firsthand, sometimes daily, the unfairness of life playing out right in front of me. Just because we pray for something and it doesn't happen doesn't mean God wants us to quit hoping.

Many of us ask ourselves: When a crisis hits hard and is coming in for the final punch, how do we respond biblically and not emotionally? When we react emotionally, we're total messes and can't see through the trees; we beat ourselves up and tell ourselves we are not spiritual enough. I am an emotional person. I cry when balloons go up at a parade.

I cry when I am happy and when I am sad. I just plain feel deeply. I discovered through this situation with Emma and other painful times in my life that responding emotionally is biblical, it's what Jesus did, it's what David did, it's what Job did, and it's what I did.

When Jesus, Job, and David cried out to God, it didn't fall on a deaf ear. I can sleep, knowing God is not shocked at what is happening to me. God isn't off taking a nap somewhere and wakes up, decides to check his Facebook, and realizes your child just died. He comes alongside us in our suffering.[8]

Their suffering did not surprise God, and ours doesn't either. God didn't expect Job, Jesus, Paul, or even Thomas to pretend things felt fantastic. He didn't expect them to hide their emotions from him. The tricky part is what we do after we call out to God, cry our heart out, and allow the questions and feelings to surface. What did Jesus do? What did David do? What did Job do? They moved through emotions and put their trust solely in God. They rejoiced in their suffering. We have to do the same thing! This is quite a tall order, at least for me.

Dear friends, do not be surprised at the fiery ordeal that has come on you to test you, as though something strange were happening to you. But rejoice inasmuch as you participate in the sufferings of Christ, so that you may be overjoyed when his glory is revealed (1 Peter 4:12-13 NIV).

When Paul talks about rejoicing in our suffering, he doesn't ask us to throw a party and say, "My close friend just died, hooray I get to suffer like Christ. Hallelujah." The Bible makes it clear that rejoicing in suffering doesn't mean pretending to be fine and getting through it. It's not being strong enough to handle anything or the ability to keep a smile on our faces and not burden anyone with our pain. Some people believe trying to be happy when bad happens makes them somehow an obedient Christian. It does not. God knows we aren't going to enjoy tribulation.

SEEK AND YOU SHALL FIND

I found hope again; I found my way out of the fire. Mark Wahlberg would be proud.

Praise be to the God and Father of our Lord Jesus Christ! In his great mercy, he has given us new birth into a living hope through the resurrection of Jesus Christ from the dead, and into an inheritance that can never perish, spoil or fade. This inheritance is kept in heaven for you, who through faith are shielded by God's power until the coming of the salvation that is ready to be revealed in the last time. In all this you greatly rejoice, though now for a little while you may have had to suffer grief in all kinds of trials. These have come so that the proven genuineness of your faith—of greater worth than gold, which perishes even though refined by fire— may result in praise, glory and honor when Jesus Christ is revealed (1 Peter 1:3-7).

God spoke to me in an inner audible voice on the porch swing, and he does continue to speak to me that way, but it's not the only way.[9] Habakkuk knew the sound of God speaking to him.[10] Elijah described it as a still, small voice.[11] I have had God's thoughts come to me in words, chapters, monologues, and sentences.

I have had God's thoughts arise in flowing spur-of-the-moment ideas, visions, and even dreams.[12] I try to write words from him down often. Suffering can be a path for all of us that leads to healing.[13] Hearing from God is vital to enjoying his eternal plan for our lives. Listening to God is our choice, and we must make that decision for ourselves. I know through Christ and the power of the Holy Spirit, God spoke to me.

I also believe God wants to speak to you the same way. I know firsthand that God wants to be involved in the smallest of details of our lives. Today, I can't survive without hearing his voice. I acknowledge him in all my ways, and he directs my path. His calling to me is unique, and I must be continuously directed by him to fulfill it.[14]

We are told in the Bible that to enter the kingdom, we must become as little children. I can do this by just remembering. God has given me such powerful landmarks in my life—landmarks that guide me home to him every time.

What landmarks has he given you? What wonderful things has God shown you in your past? What whispers of encouragement do you hear? He is speaking; I guarantee it!

When I become like a little child, I hear God, my friend, and I chatting it up while we swing back and forth, back and forth on the porch swing.[15] I instantly see the truth of his voice and all the possibilities ahead. When I look back at my childhood, I see myself running through the flames into the arms of Jesus.

EIGHT

WILD HORSES

Have you ever gone to buy a desk chair? You don't just look at it; you sit on it, push on it, and move it up and down while pressure testing it. You want to see if the chair will withstand what you have planned for it. Will this chair be able to take the long hours of you sitting on it?

In the same way, God wants to make sure we are up for the task and purpose he has planned for us as well. At times, he must get us ready, so we can be stronger in him, not only to get through unbearable trials but also to stand up under them and then be up for the great and mighty plan he has planned for us.[16]

God knows firsthand what it's like to suffer.[17] The Bible shows us Jesus enduring great suffering when others despised, spit on, betrayed, ridiculed, and crucified him. They put him on trial, rejected him, and tempted him. He did not deserve what happened to him, and often, we don't deserve what happens to us.

He withstood suffering to fulfill God's purpose. He suffered not for his sins but for ours.[18] Through Christ's suffering, he made our salvation possible. Amen. Jesus was a man of sorrows acquainted with grief.[19] I keep that written in my phone on my notes, and whenever the darkness threatens to close in on me, I read it. It helps me to re-

member that God knows what grief feels like. It helps remind me God knows what I feel like.

Committed to knowing and obeying God's written Word
already, during this time, I had to take it a step farther and
meditate on Scriptures over and over again.[20] I had to re-
plant God's truth in my heart. God dwells in our hearts, and
because we can hear God speaking to us, we can take steps
in faith and obedience toward God's leading. I began to
make decisions based on what I believe God showed me,
told me, and wanted for me other than what I thought or
felt.

THOUGHT TRAIN

Maybe the sheer evil of what Emma did or the demonic
support she had is what kept coming to me and attacking
me right in the middle of my prayer time, my worship time,
my walk time, and my every time. Or maybe Satan ordered
the attack. I knew all the reasoning in my mind came from
me. I knew good thoughts came from the Holy Spirit, and I
knew—without a shadow of a doubt—unprompted evil
thoughts came straight from hell. During this period of darkness, I wandered aimlessly in my negative thoughts.

I tried so hard to tune into what I heard and trust God,
but Satan wasn't just going to retreat quietly. Satan wasn't
going to say, "Sorry I hurt you, Tracy, I will leave you alone
now." As I sat in the aftermath of Emma's delivered
schemes, Satan's thoughts came in like a freight train, so I
had to take every thought captive [2 Cor. 10:5].

One way I think of 2 Corinthians and taking my every
thought captive is like this: I think of a large pen packed full
of hundreds and hundreds of wild horses. I imagine what

might happen if all of a sudden the gate to the pen accidently opened, and all of the wild horses escaped. Horses were running free everywhere. I think of the possible destruction, not to mention the difficulty in rounding them up again.

Now, I picture my thoughts, especially negative ones, as those same horses. Every day our minds are flooded with a never-ending stream of negative thoughts: doubt, guilt, worries, fear, and so on. While any one of these thoughts can make us feel overwhelmed and defeated, the truth is we are often inundated with more than one.

Our minds are packed full of hundreds to thousands of thoughts that are just waiting for any opportunity to be let loose and ultimately cause much destruction in our lives. Satan wants us worn out, wrung out, and ready for nothing. He wants to steal all of our joy and leave us feeling empty, full of questions, and bombarded with reasoning.

He wants us defeated, discouraged, depressed, and despondent. Our everyday life is a daily battle of fighting the war to take every thought captive to Christ.

We demolish arguments and every pretension that sets itself up against the knowledge of God, and we take captive every thought to make it obedient to Christ (2 Cor. 10:5).

We must win this war. If we take all of our thoughts captive to Christ, especially damaging and destructive ones, we can prevent a lot of pain, discomfort, distress, anxiety, and many other undesirable feelings. Deep feelings can be beautiful when we are showing compassion and giving mercy. When we allow negative thoughts to invade our feelings to the point we can't round them up, we can get lost in pain and stuck in defeat.

When a wild horse gets loose, we must immediately go after it if we ever have a chance of catching it. If a negative thought sets itself up against us, we too must immediately go after it. We must not let bad thoughts, one after another, run rampant, destroying our hearts and lives. It is much easier to gather up one loose horse than it is to try to gather up a hundred horses and get them back into a pen.

The key is not to let any of our thoughts run loose, which is no easy task. Admittedly, I am still learning this. When a negative thought pops up in my mind, such as, "I am no good," "What if?"... "I bet I have cancer," "I will never get well," "No one really cares about me," "God doesn't see me," "God doesn't love me," "I can't trust God," I must try to instantly turn that negative thought into a positive one.

With practice, we can immediately reframe that negative thought into a positive one using God's Word. It may not be easy at first, but you will get the hang of it. "God made me and he doesn't make mistakes," "God loves my child and nothing is impossible for him," "By his stripes, I am healed," "God loves me!" "God sees me" "I can do anything in this life with God by my side." "I can trust God to take care of me."

We must get our thoughts in alignment with what God says in his Word. Don't be deceived into believing those negative thoughts. Don't receive one word from Satan. Send it back where it came from. We must silence Satan in our thought life and begin to trust God again. Decide today to get into the habit of taking back your thoughts and putting them back in the pen—captive to Christ. The truth set me free, and it shall set you free as well.

The Bible presents a lot of detailed instructions on what kinds of things we should think about. Philippians 4:8 tells us to think about things that build us up, not tear us down.

For the rest, brethren, whatever is true, whatever is worthy of reverence and is honorable and seemly, whatever is just, whatever is pure, whatever is lovely and lovable, whatever is kind and winsome and gracious, if there is any virtue and excellence, if there is anything worthy of praise, think on and weigh and take account of these things."

The more time we devote to thinking about the Word, the more power and ability we will have to walk in it. I journal this scripture daily. I write down the words such as: true, just, honorable, lovely, pure, winsome, gracious, and so on. I then write under each word what is true, what is lovely, what is excellent. It is a great way to think and take account of the things of God.

In the weeks and months following Emma's confession, thousands of horses got loose and were running wild in my mind. So many unanswered questions plagued me. The constant attempt to dismember her story and figure out all of what Emma did brought so many thoughts. I turned into a horse whisperer. I had to tightly hold onto the soothing, reassuring, comforting, pure, kind, gentle, healing, life-giving, and full of mercy thoughts.[21]

All the critical, condemning, negative, hurtful, accusing, fearful destructive, and thoughts of doubt needed to be rounded up and sent back to the pen.[22] I knew I needed a quiet place to sort through all the madness, but I couldn't still my thoughts and emotions for days. I wanted so badly to be still.[23]

NINE

ARISING FROM HOPELESSNESS

The Greek word for suffering is translated as "tribula-tion." Tribulation in the dictionary is one pretty strong noun. The definition says it's a cause or state of great trouble or suffering. Synonyms: suffering, distress, trouble, misery, wretchedness, unhappiness, sadness, heartache, woe, grief, sorrow, pain, anguish, agony, trouble difficulty, problem, worry, anxiety, burden, cross to bear, ordeal, trial, adversity, hardship, tragedy, trauma, affliction, or setback.

As soon as I wrote all these synonyms down, I wanted to go running far away from tribulation. Then I learned what tribulation could produce in my heart and life and rethought my position.

> *And not only this, but we also exult in our tribula-tions, knowing that tribulation brings about persever-ance; and perseverance, proven character; and proven character, hope; and hope does not disap-point, because the love of God has been poured out within our hearts through the Holy Spirit who was given to us* (Romans 5:3-5).

Tribulation brings perseverance, perseverance brings proven character, and proven character brings hope. It's crazy that we need character, and we all desperately want hope in our lives. Without hope, our lives are empty scary places. How can we be so hopeless *during* our suffering only to produce hope *through* our suffering?

So no hope equals hope. That's a math equation that doesn't make any sense or seems to have the right answer. You think, How can I understand this? Well, don't go to Bible school to find out, because you won't find your answer there. We find our answers when we don't panic, and instead, persevere.

When we pray for spiritual strength, God shows up. When we stay under the pressure and begin to suffer long enough, we can get steadier and stronger. God does want to test us. He wants to see if we are up to our salt and if we will trust him. He wants us to hope.

A MIRAGE

At the age of three, my son Adam drowned. He stopped breathing. His eyes fixed, his pupils dilated, and he went to the bathroom in his pants. I can remember when I had to call 911, the operator kept asking me, "What's the matter? Ma'am, what is your emergency?"

Only one word came to my mind, "Jesus, Jesus, Jesus, Jesus, Jesus." I had no other thought in my head. The operator had no idea why I did not respond to her. I knew it was too late, and I knew the only person who could help him or me was Jesus.

Adam remained this way for at least twenty minutes, maybe more. My son died. My pastor, who lived ten miles away, got the word my son had drowned via phone call. He drove over to my house, and when he got there, my son Adam was still not breathing. You can take your mouse and scroll through Google, and you will find over and over that within three to five minutes of not breathing, the brain will suffer serious damage.

As they loaded my son's lifeless body in the ambulance, shock and horror filled the streets around us. This just couldn't be happening. Thoughts like firecrackers exploded in my mind, "He has aspirated. He's brain dead. My precious little three year old can't be gone!" My bright and beautiful son's eyes looked dark and empty. He didn't smile back at me or respond to my voice. Frantically, I got in the ambulance with him, and it began to make its way to a local hospital.

I am not sure if you have had anyone die in front of you. Often when people die, they take weird breaths. When I worked in the hospital, we called them death breaths. It's something the body does when it's dying. My son's body began those breaths. He didn't take long breaths in and out; instead, he made tiny little squeaks. He did not respond or breathe normally; he just made these weird, irregular, short, and awful sounds.

Then all of a sudden, and I mean in an instant, he miraculously awoke in the ambulance as if nothing had happened to him and began speaking to me. It seemed like he just woke up from a nap. He said, "Hi, Mom." He pointed out the window and began talking about the preschool he was to attend the next day. I couldn't believe my eyes!

We arrived at the hospital, and they found no water in his lungs and no sign of drowning afterward. My daughter Amanda is five years older than Adam. She was playing at school while this happened, and shockingly, we made it home from the hospital before she got home from school—

talk about a whirlwind of trauma and hope all batched together like cookie dough. It took months to recover.

People said, "Why are you struggling? Adam didn't die." As a young Christian, I attended a church at the time that taught principles like when something bad happens, we must have done something to bring it on. Maybe I didn't pray enough or have enough faith etc. I have since learned how bad theology messes with us; nonetheless, I wrestled giants to find understanding.

I thought about parents who did not get to take their child home from the hospital. I now knew how every parent felt when they lost a child, and I grieved for them. I overprotected Adam and Amanda as a result of my ongoing fear. Because of all the screams in my house that day, I allowed no one to scream for at least a year.

Fear moved in lock, stock, and barrel. From then on, I tried to do everything right by God in an attempt to be safe. I kept thinking, *Why let him die and then come back?* I felt like I owed God for answering my prayers. Have you ever felt like that? I felt like he warned me. Don't misunderstand; I was also deeply grateful! I gave every second I had to God and my family. I just walked on ice for years after this accident. Afraid. I lived in fear of making a mistake, any mistake that could potentially jeopardize my children's lives.

Poor kids! They could barely play outside, spend the night anywhere, or eat carrots because I thought they would choke. No way did I allow them to do any sports or anything dangerous. If they ate meat, it had to be completely cut up. When the time came to ride their bikes or anything that posed a danger, the regimen started with putting on the pads. First came the helmet, then the knee pads, then the elbow pads, and at times, gloves. Long pants and long sleeves made the list too.

The kids would cry, "Mom, it's too tight. I can't breathe; I'm choking!" The bike wobbled, and they could barely see outside of all their gear, but I did not care because I did my part to keep them safe. And it didn't stop there. I put locks on the doors, sticks in the windows to prevent their opening, and took a billion trips to the doctor if they even sneezed. I prayed every second for God to please take care of them. As such a young Christian, I had no real understanding of the Bible or how God and the Bible fit together.

I remembered the God from the porch swing, and I knew without a shadow of a doubt the reality of God. I knew deep down that he loved me, but that knowledge and the feelings I tried balancing from the accident did not reconcile. When the boogeyman is hiding around every corner waiting to hurt your children, and you are running around looking for him every second, exhaustion takes over.

Listen, I loved my kids. I loved my husband. I couldn't bear the thought of losing them. The day my son drowned proved to be the day I learned of the real possibility one of my kids could die in front of me, and the day I decided not to let that happen.

MY PROVISION

Two years later, my mother suddenly died at the age of fifty-nine. She died in my arms as I did CPR. After her death, I sat for hours upon hours, mourning the loss of my mother in my most sacred place—my porch swing hanging in the front of my house. Back and forth I went. I was beside myself with pain, shock, fright, and discontentment.

Then something beautiful happened. Earlier that day, I paced in the kitchen and cried in shock and disbelief. Hysteria overtook me. I kept asking my husband Mike, "Where was my provision?" Over the last couple of years, I had grown a lot as a Christian. My relationship flourished with God, and I had learned to trust him and applied his Word all over my life. I said to Mike, "I know my God, and I know his word and I know he says I will have my provision (I needed it and wanted it)."[24] I knew my mom belonged to Jesus, and I understood he loved her. At the same time, I saw him as my heavenly Father who not only gave her to me, he allowed me to love her and knew how much I desperately needed her.

My parents waited ten years for a baby. When they adopted me, I weighed in at four pounds, and they spoiled me rotten every day after. (My mom and dad were married 43 years when she died.) She loved me unconditionally and with every bit of her soul. So now with her suddenly gone, I felt alone and sad. I did not question God. I thankfully did not get angry. My husband said to me, "God will give you your provision; he is faithful, and he will give you your provision." I waited.

Back to the porch swing. I went and continued swinging as the wood held comfortably under me. I contemplated the whole situation, and no matter how I framed this turn of events, peace eluded me.

When someone you love dies, it shines a huge light on whatever cracks you have in your faith. Everyone told me she was in heaven and she was better off. Friends said, "She's happy." How could she be happy? She would never want to leave me. Everyone talked about heaven as a magical place, and at that moment, I grew so sick of hearing it. I am sorry, but I needed to know exactly where she went. Where was her sweet spirit, her soul—where was she? Heaven did not mean anything to me. For some reason, heaven seemed more like a word than a place. Although I became a Christian so many years before this and am a pastor now, at this moment, heaven turned into such a cliché. I missed her.

I felt like the best years of my life ended, and now my life became a chore to endure. A day or so later, as I pondered this almost to my physical and mental demise, I had a thought. It came to me like a streak of lightning. Adam my son had died—but where did he go?

GO BACK

Adam drowned at age three. A few months after the drowning, we were driving along, and a Crystal Lewis song played on the radio. I heard her words singing, "God is good to me." From his car seat, my son said aloud, "Mom, God is good to me, huh?"

I said, "Yes, son."

"He flew me around and just dropped me in the ambulance."

"What?"

"You know, you were there." This was the first I heard of anything like this. We kept singing, and I didn't pry or push the subject. A year or so later, we must have been talking about God, and he said, "Mom, I did not see God. I only saw his hands and feet." Again I didn't ask more questions. I remember encouragement raced through me. Knowing his young age and innocence, I wanted to protect this memory and make sure neither my husband nor I ever put any words in his mouth.

As I sat on the swing with my husband after my mom's death, I asked my husband to bring my son to me. His now five-year-old frame fit neatly in my husband's arms when he carried him over. I asked my son to close his eyes. He appeared frightened.

He recognized my hysteria and wanted me to be okay. He sometimes seemed like a thirty-year-old man, and I seemed like the five-year-old child. He always had and still does have such great wisdom. His honesty always touched my heart. He closed his eyes, and I asked him if he remembered when he drowned.

"Ya, God picked me up and flew me around and dropped me in the ambulance."

"No, back up. You were playing with Alex (a little boy, son of the cleaning lady who spoke no English), and you decided to go around to the back gate to splash water on Alex." This back gate never opened; it remained stuck shut for years. In fact, we threw the key to the front pool gate in the trash. If you wanted to mow the yard, you needed to carry the mower over the fence. There was no entrance to the pool without climbing, or so we thought. Unbeknownst to us, the back gate had blown open in the ninety mile an hour winds we had experienced the day before.

"No, Mom," he said. Well, you need to know how shocked I felt at this moment. What did he mean no? We always thought that he spied a crack in the gate that blew open and decided to go around the driveway and splash water on his friend and fell in. "No, Mom. I went around the house, and when I put the broom in the water to get a toy out, I fell in." It was apparent he vividly remembered what had happened.

"Okay, you fell in. Then what happened?" He said he tried to swim, and he yelled for his dad in his mind. He said he waited for my husband to come and get him. He said he kept trying to get out. "Then what?" He was silent. "Adam, did you go to a place like Chuck E. Cheese, a place like the park, or did you just wait and then wake up in the ambulance?"

"I went to a place." He looked up with his eyes open as if to be staring at something (not looking at me), his eyes mesmerized. At the age of three, he couldn't articulate what happened, now he not only articulated what happened, he sat there looking straight at it.

I said, "That place is where Nana is."

He got kind of upset and said, "If Nana is there, why did you tell Amanda (his sister) she passed away?" He looked at me and said, "Mom, she did not pass away! If you knew where she went, why didn't you tell Amanda that?"

"That place where you were, the place where you went, son, that's heaven," I said.

Realizing my son had seen and been to heaven, my insides burst with questions. "Was it green there?"

"No, Mom." I just wanted to jump into his eyes. I sat there so puzzled because we always think of heaven as green pastures.

"What color was it?

"Mostly gold...like golden fields or something."

"Well, Nana has been there now, and she has seen it, and you know how much Nana loved me?"

"Yes," he said.

"Would she want to come back now?"

"No." He knew I didn't want to hear that answer, yet he told his truth.

"No?"

"No," he repeated.

"Did you want to come back?"

"No." He looked very baffled when he said this—like he was thinking, *Why am I here?*

"Why did you come back?"

"I don't know."

"Did people know your name?" I asked.

"Yes."

"Were people smiling?"

"Yes."

"Was there blue there?"

"Yes, Mom," he said, and then he pointed at my sweatshirt, which was cobalt blue. "That color blue." He said again that he did not see God but only saw his hands and feet.

"Will Nana like it there?"

"No, she will love it there."

HE SAW HEAVEN. THE PLACE.

I could never possibly understand the day my son drowned, what significance his drowning would have on my life. Had my son not been able to tell me what he did that day, I may have never recovered. God knew that too. God used the tragedy of my son's drowning to bring me my provision.[25] He knew Adam was the only person I could've heard those words from.

For so many months, I thought I did something that didn't please God to cause such a brutal trial in my life. In reality, God knew exactly what I needed. I saw Adam die in front of me. I had to—otherwise, I would never have believed it. Then, when I approached the verge of literally dying inside, Adam's death brought me life.

I love it when God takes a sharpie marker and draws a huge black circle around something in our lives. He brought it all back full circle. He gave me true beauty for ashes.[26]

ONE BIG SWOOP OF GOD'S HAND

Then the Lord said to Joshua, "Command the priests carrying the ark of the covenant law to come up out of the Jordan." So Joshua commanded the priests, "Come up out of the Jordan. And the priests came up out of the river carrying the ark of the covenant of the Lord. No sooner had they set their feet on the dry ground than the waters of the Jordan returned to their place and ran at flood stage as before. On the tenth day of the first month the people went up from the Jordan and camped at Gilgal on the eastern border of Jericho. And Joshua set up at Gilgal the twelve stones they had taken out of the Jordan. He said to the Israelites, "In the future when your descendants ask their parents, 'What do these stones mean?' tell them, 'Israel crossed the Jordan on dry ground' For the Lord your God dried up the Jordan before you until you had crossed over. The Lord your God did to the Jordan what he had done to the Red Sea when he dried it up before us until we had crossed over. He did this so that all the peoples of the earth might know that the hand of the Lord is powerful and so that you might always fear the Lord your God" (Joshua 4:15-22 NIV).

The Israelites wandered in the wilderness for forty years. Then God made a huge move and dried up the Jordan River to allow the Israelites a path into the Promised Land. Joshua led them across that dry river, and suddenly, the Promised Land stood under their feet. Can you imagine after forty years of waiting and wandering, probably thinking it was never going to happen, abruptly, with one big swoop of God's hand, you're delivered!

Gilgal is a place located between Jordan and Jericho. It's the place where Joshua set up camp after they all crossed the Jordan River. A representative from each of the twelve tribes of Israel took one stone from the riverbed and made a memorial in Gilgal. They placed this memorial there to remind generations to come of God's mighty deliverance.

In the Hebrew text, Gilgal means a circle (of stones), which is perfect because it is right where the Israelites came full circle in receiving God's rescue and freedom.

We too have moments just like this. For me, I have the porch swing, Adam's drowning, and the amazing provision God provided for me through his drowning after my mom's death. God is a God of miracles! God has taken me from dry, brittle places where I blindly wandered and miraculously brought me full circle to fresh streams of living water. He has brought me healing and restoration when I thought it wasn't possible.

FULL CIRCLE MOMENTS

Jesus Christ is the same yesterday as he is today.[27] Emma robbed us of many things, ruined relationships, and caused extreme damage with her sick plot. Emma revealed her seven-year-old abuse story just days before Christmas.

This had left us heartbroken and grieving and made it practically impossible to enjoy our holiday as a family.

Mike and I lost touch with many of our friends and family during the time we supposedly helped her bring down child pornographers. She drove my car all the time, so every time I looked at my car after the truth came out, I thought of her. The ministry where I work lost great girls who loved the Lord and the ministry. I never read a book the whole time. This may sound small, but for me, this is HUGE. Mike and I were disconnected and didn't get to see one another at all.

She pretended to be my FBI therapist and messed with my head. But God is the God of miracles. In one second, He can bring a full circle moment to bring freedom and rescue.

In the aftermath, I called my friends I hadn't spoken to in months, and many awesome reunions took place. I loved seeing their smiles and faces again. I rehired every girl intentionally driven out of the ministry, and they have flourished beyond my wildest dreams. I followed up with my friend and therapist, Michelle. I am doing great!

I processed all the images from my PTSD and have moved past my grief. Frankly, I am better than I have ever been! I broke the stronghold of fear in my life. Praise God! I got a great new car. Mike and I took a fantastic trip together. I have a stack of books I have read! I am happy to report we had a spectacular Christmas the following year. Every family member joined us, even our grandkids from out of state. God brought these things and so many other things right back to us.

Every day I get a new revelation of God's hand during the time I thought God's closeness left me. I have had new visions, dreams, and creativity abounding in me. He has given me double for my former trouble.[28] He continues to restore all she managed to ruin temporarily, and we are reclaiming all God has for us every second. Take this book, for example—a terrible story of pain but a beautiful ending of love.

Jesus doesn't waste one tear we ever shed. Our stories are never wasted, not even the bad ones. He can take what we think is the darkest hour of our lives and transform it into the brightest, lightest moment of our existence if we will let him.

It can be so hard to see the big picture God sees when we only see pain. It can be so difficult to trust him and believe he knows what he is doing. No matter how much we know about God, we all feel we have limited knowledge. The Word of God is alive, and each time we open it up and read, we discover new things.

If, for a moment, we can begin looking for the things God would have us looking for instead of every other thing that sets itself up against God, we can find new levels of peace and wholeness.[29] Yes, the world is a dark place, and at times, we might feel like we are wandering alone in the wilderness. But God has a plan for us just like he did for the Israelites. He has provision waiting right around the corner. We may walk through real darkness, but God doesn't expect us not to hurt while we are there.

He expects us to hope.

TEN

STUCK ON THE BUS

The thing with suffering is, we all hate it. I can't think of one person who says, "Yay, more discomfort, please," or "Pass the agony." I do not wish to ask for second helpings of it, nor did I ever ask for the first helping. Let's face it, when the pain hits, we brace ourselves like when we get the stomach flu. We hang on for dear life, believing that this distress will pass. The flu lasts for a while and then leaves. Grief and sadness come in waves and then go.[30] Time does heal.

When the flu is finally over, the last thing I want to do is remember every detail of what made me feel so sick. Similarly, when the grief begins to pass or the shock and horror of a heartbreak fade, the last thing I want to do is re-experience every minute of the melancholy. But what do I tend to do? I get stuck on the bus! I re-live the distress all over again and again. I rewind every aspect in my mind and try to reason my way back through it. I keep staring at my anguish like a pinwheel, eyes bulging, not blinking, as it spins around and around my mind. Why do I do this? Why do we do this? Why are we so content to regurgitate every dreadful thing that has ever happened?

We are perfectly happy to ruminate on everyone's offenses, doom, dread, and pain, especially our own. If we can figure out what transpired—I mean retrace our steps and figure out why things ensued—maybe we could prevent the same thing from taking us down in the future.

Every night Emma insisted on wearing a black hoodie to bed. Every night she awoke in a memory, crying and biting the sleeves of this sweatshirt, desperately trying to get out of it. This sweatshirt triggered a memory where one of her assailants strapped her in a straightjacket then assaulted her. Every night I said, "Emma, take that off! Please do not wear that. If you do, we will be up all night long while you rip and tear at it, and then I'll have to work for an hour to get it off of you." I figured not wearing the sweatshirt to bed would prevent pain.

In the same way, when the Emma thing ended, I worked hard to try to figure out why it happened. Did I let my guard down? Was I too trusting? What changes could I make that would prevent me from ever getting entangled with a crazy person again? There could be a speck of truth in this approach. If we could see why something happened to us, maybe we could avoid certain things in anticipation of preventing further pain.

Beyond that, I think we just feel better when we can identify something. I know I do. We make lots of cognitive assumptions in our mind as to why things occurred and then move forward, happily putting new protective boundaries in place, boundaries we probably didn't even need. I am quite positive my kids did not need the excessive padding I made them wear daily.

Are we helping ourselves? Maybe you had a brutal car accident on a windy road near your home. To protect yourself from this ever happening again, you may make the decision to never drive that road in the future. However, chances are, you could drive that road the rest of your life and never have another accident there.

Some might go even further and choose never to drive again or never leave the house. Chances are you could drive the rest of your life and never have another accident any-where, yet, we feel we must do something to protect our-selves from further misery. So we act out in our fear and distress and make poor choices. I made plenty.

Pain has a way of making a permanent home in our memories. Even when we try to forget the upsets of long ago and move on, we can't. The old excruciating memories of the past beg us to spend time with them in our present. Unfortunately, we give in to their demands.

We can't keep concentrating on our past pain, failures, actions, and hopes. One day I got a call from the front desk, and they said I had a pastor-on-call appointment for that day. Later on, a very distraught middle-aged woman walked into my office. I greeted her, and after she sat down, I asked her, "What's wrong?"

She said, "Do you mind if I start at the beginning?"

I said, "No, go ahead." She took out a stack of papers.

"Do you mind if I read it to you? It's difficult to talk about."

"No, feel free." I thought she must have had something terrible just happen.

She began reading her papers, and to my surprise, she started her story some forty—yes, forty—years prior. She sat in my office sobbing and brokenhearted about things that had happened forty years ago. She got stuck in the past, and it ruined years of her life.

She kept asking me questions such as, "Do you think if I

spoke up that day when I was ten things would be different?" This went on for a couple of hours.

STUCK ON THE BUS

Picture yourself on a school bus, and no, this is not one of those games where at the end, I ask you who drove the bus. You're a child getting ready to exit the bus to go home after school where there are countless after-school snacks, welcoming family, abounding love, and the smells of dinner cooking, steadfast support, and safety.

Each day you exit the bus with a great big hope in your heart, childlike anticipation, and expectations of the splendor waiting for you beyond the bus doors. One day you get off the bus, walk home, and a very unexpected, horrifying thing happens. (You can insert your own terrible thing here.)

In the days to follow, you hesitate to exit the bus. When it's time to get off the bus, you think about what it used to be like. You focus on the past first, the good things, and then the bad. You can't shake the fact that you don't feel full of expectation anymore. You have lost that childlike faith, and your hope is now gone too. Fear, dread, and worry have filled your mind. As the bus approaches your regular stop, you feel sick. You have lots of regrets. You think that if you hadn't gone to school the day of the terrible thing, things would be different. You think perhaps it's all your fault that the awful thing took place. You are homesick for what used to be.

You hope for the best but prepare for the worst because you don't want to be disappointed or surprised by another bad thing. You find yourself stuck on the bus, not wanting to get off anymore. You decide to just stay put. At first, when the driver took you to your stop and even other stops, you peeked out the door to see if you felt ready to exit. Then you decided no, not yet, and then put your head back in.

You just sat in the front seat of the bus riding around and around, not exiting. As the days go by, you stop putting your head out. Every time you tried to put your head out, the memories of the past came flooding back. And the closer you got to the exit, the more uncomfortable you became. You decided to move one seat back to protect yourself from the pain. As you started your journey back, it didn't stop. Now you're seated at the back of the bus. You figure it's safer back there. You're the farthest from the bus doors that you can get—farther from the chance of ever having to exit and experience the kind of discomfort you did before.

People are still riding the bus. You see them getting on and off the bus, and you wish you rode the bus as easily with no fear and apprehension. As time continues to go by, some great people got on the bus with you; they spent time with you, and you liked it. However, they eventually had to go home.

You know you must get off the bus, but you don't know how to do it. You figure maybe if you move up one seat at a time, you will be ready to make the long voyage down the bus steps.

I am here to tell you it's time to exit the bus. I'm not talking about moving up one seat at a time, then putting your hand out the doors to test the outside. I am not talking about making a slow descent down the aisle. I am recommending right now that you run up the center aisle and burst through those doors. We can do things when we are afraid, and this is courageous. I don't want you just to be brave; I want you to hope again.

I want you to fill your head with hopes and dreams. It's a risk, I know Proverbs 13:12 says, "Hope deferred makes the heart sick but when the dream is realized it's like a tree of life." You can hope for the best but expect the worst, which is not hoping for the best.

It's as if you are expecting the bad thing; but if the good happens to occur, you're happy. This is different than hoping for the best thing; and if a bad thing by some slim chance happens, you are surprised and walk through as it happens with God right next to you.

You can hope for the big things, the big dreams, the little dreams, and with bold expectation begin looking and waiting for them to happen. If you expect the worst, and a good thing happens, you get to enjoy that good thing. If you expect the best and the best happens, you get to not only enjoy the best thing that happened but, according to the word of God, you get a tree of life.

Doesn't that sound astounding? A tree of life? The Bible also tells us hope deferred makes the heart sick. If you defer your hope just waiting to see if you can be excited and if God decides to do something good for you, you are deferring your hope. We can't give up on our hopes. Sometimes when what we are hoping for doesn't happen soon enough, we get weary, sad, and just stop hoping.

Sometimes we hope big and get disappointed. But at least our hearts won't be sick. The trick is to hope for more things, important things that can change our lives and others' lives for the better.

It's kind of like gambling. The more numbers you put

your chips on, the better chance you have for your number to come in. Let's see, we can hope for a great dinner, a good day at work, a child getting better, a nice lunch, or a friend to have dinner with.

As we go on, we can hope for bigger and bigger and bigger. If the thing we're hoping for seems to have disappeared, we need to hope for more things. The goal is to live in the constant shade of the tree of life. I get it, we truly are afraid to feel the kind of pain again that drove us to the back of the bus in the first place. We can discern victories of the past, but it is futile for us to live in the great yesteryears, trying to figure out exactly why things happened the way they did. It's futile for us to keep trying to protect ourselves. The bus can't protect us, and we can't protect ourselves. Only God can protect us. Our cages are not locked, and we are not doomed to live in the past. See Psalm 124:7-8 (NIV). We can spend so much time looking back at our past that we don't spend enough time envisioning our future.

HAVE YOU EVER SHOT A BIRD?

When my son Adam reached about fifteen, he got a brand new BB gun. Afterwards, he invited all of his friends, who also had guns, to our house to do some shooting. After a long day of shooting targets and other things like apples, bottles, cans, and even one of my lanterns, Adam came to me with a question.

"Mom, what would you think if I shot a bird?"

"Well, son," I said, "I like birds, and I just don't understand why people want to shoot any animals.

"Yeah," he said and sat there a minute, looking out the window. "I asked Bompa [Grandpa] if he ever shot a bird, and he said yes. When he found the dead bird, he said he started crying like a baby and felt so bad. Then I asked Dad if he ever shot a bird, and he said yes. Dad said that afterwards he just felt horrible!"

"Wow, I didn't know that," I said, "but I bet I would feel awful too!"

Adam pondered that for quite awhile, and then to my surprise, he announced in a resigned voice, "Okay, Mom, I guess I'll go shoot a bird."

"What?" I exclaimed. His statement floored me. *Did he not hear a word I said? Will he really shoot a bird?*

"Well, someday my son is going to come and ask me, 'Dad, have you ever shot a bird, and what's it like?' And, Mom, I'm going to need an answer for him."

This is such a great story on many levels. First, it's amazing a fifteen-year-old boy is thinking beyond the moment, especially about such deep subjects. What I found truly enlightening was the notion of looking at the present moment and seeing the big picture! We too must begin to look at a larger view of our future.

WATER

"The only thing worse than being blind is having sight with no vision." –*Helen Keller*

As a child, I watched the movie *The Miracle Worker.* The film is a true story about a woman named Anne Sullivan and her struggle to teach a blind and deaf child named Helen Keller to communicate.

Helen Keller's personality overflowed with rebelliousness, her spirit stronger than any I have ever seen. As a baby, she lost her sight and hearing after she contracted scarlet fever. As Helen grew up, she became increasingly exasperated at her inability to communicate with others.

She had ferocious flare-ups, and her parents could not even begin to control her. They had absolutely no idea what to do with her. They got in contact with the Perkins School for the Blind to help them learn how to deal with Helen. The school provided a tutor named Anne Sullivan.

Anne consistently went to Helen's home. She worked diligently with Helen in an attempt to teach her how to communicate. She wanted Helen to be able to get the things she needed like food and water without having to throw a fit.

They fought and fought, and Helen strongly resisted her efforts at first, but Anne didn't give up. She stayed the course with Helen and not only taught her table manners, but also how to speak with her hands and her heart. I remember when Helen said her first word, "WATER!" I can still picture that powerful scene. Can you imagine having all of your feelings bottled up inside you for years and being unable to express them? Then one day it clicks, and all of a sudden, you can communicate. She learned to tell her parents how she felt about them. She learned to read in braille. Her life opened up. Once Helen expressed her thoughts and feelings, she never stopped communicating them.[31]

I admire Helen Keller beyond words. She fascinates me to no end. She saw beyond her current circumstances, had high ambition despite her disabilities, and showed colossal courage against overwhelming odds. She spent her whole life helping, inspiring, teaching, and loving others. She made a conscious choice to stop looking at the bad hand dealt to her.

She stopped focusing on what she couldn't do and instead put a laser focus on what she could do. She did not let the pain of her past dictate her future. She began looking for hope and found it. She got a new vision for her life and lived her dreams in full color in front of millions, blessing millions along the way.

WHAT'S GOD'S VISION FOR YOUR LIFE?

A vision is a clear and concise image of the future as it can and should be. It is an extensive mental portrait of what tomorrow can and will look like—a complete view of the future and its exciting potential. (See *Developing a Vision for Ministry in the 21st Century* by Aubrey Malphurs.)

We all must have a strong vision for our lives. What mental portrait do you have in your mind? Is it a portrait of yesterday or tomorrow? We can say much about living in today, but the benefits of hoping for and picturing our bright futures remain important, too. Vision is crucial. A vision is not a dream, it's not goals and objectives, it's not a purpose, and it's not a mission. Vision is always cast in terms of the future.

We hear a lot today about mission statements. Churches, families, even individuals are making them. While a mission helps people *know* where they are going, a vision allows them to actually *see* where they are going. God has given me fresh vision over the years in many areas of my life. Take this book, for example. I believe God spoke clearly and told me to write it.

I resisted at first. Then he continued to prompt me and lead me in the right direction. He gave me the name first. Then he showed me visions, stories, if you will, that went right along with my story. He opened doors for the book. The most important thing is he helped me write it. Every computer glitch and every painful moment I re-lived while writing it, he stayed as close to me as my own breath.

What is God's vision for you? Vision clarifies direction, invites unity, facilitates function, enhances guidance, prompts passion, fosters risk-taking, offers sustenance, creates energy, provides purpose, and can provoke radical generosity. Do you see anything?

As we learn from Nehemiah in Proverbs 29:18 (KJV), "Where there is no vision the people perish." We are perishing from a lack of vision. We must remember God has a vision for us, and he wants us to be diligent, full of passion, and equipped to carry it out. God does not want us isolated and suffering. We can't let our perspective of yesterday steal our hope and vision for our future.

We can't let our fascination with the past lead us to perish. His mercies are new every morning.[32] No matter where we have been or what we have been through, God has a plan—a plan he wishes to reveal to us. God has fresh vision and inspiration for our lives. God has things for us to do, see, and feel.

God wants us to know things that we cannot know except as revelation—as a gift of God working through the Holy Spirit. Beg God for this revelation. Keep crying out to him, keep moving forward in him to stay whole, balanced, and motivated.

ELEVEN

NINJA WARRIOR ROCKS

I woke up from a dead sleep at about three one morning, and God gave me an unexpected revelation. Have you ever woken up and wondered, first of all, *Why am I awake?* Then you wonder, *Is there something you want to show me, Lord?* Then you see something and wonder, *Is this God, or am I just imagining it?* Then you begin to go with it, and in seconds, you know this is God because you could never come up with something so well thought out and crystal clear, especially at three in the morning.

That night he gave me a clear vision of a rose tree. I saw a single pink rose standing tall, its petals delicate and fluffy, even dewy. It smelled fantastic. Then I saw the rose snipped off. It dropped to the ground with its petals falling all around. The stem was still intact, standing upright, firm, and full of thorns.

The rose tree remained planted firmly. Yet, its beauty appeared gone. Just because the beauty of the rose laid trampled on the ground, I sensed it didn't mean the rose tree went down for the count. Just because the rose itself seemed to go missing didn't mean the beauty in the rose disappeared forever. I identified immediately with this vision. After the truth came out and all of Emma's conniving and plotting exposed, I felt snipped off and flattened on the ground.

I can remember feeling so foolish. At one point, I bought a birthday present for Agent Johnson. Emma told me his favorite thing in the world was birthday cake flavored cake pops from Starbucks. So I went to Starbucks and bought 24 cake pops for him. Later that day, I texted him and told him I got him a little something for his birthday.

He texted back so excited and told me he and another agent planned on coming by the next day while we worked to pick it up. When I got home from work, he had taken the cake pops. He texted a great big thank you, left a handwritten note for me, and elaborated about how sick he felt from eating so many.

When Mike set up all the cameras, they began recording the events happening in our home. The cameras captured Emma sneaking those cake pops away from where I placed them and hiding them in my very own house. Talk about feeling snipped off.

I realized I was the rose. Maybe you are too?

Therefore be imitators of God, as beloved children; and walk in love, just as Christ also loved you and gave Himself up for us, an offering and a sacrifice to God as a fragrant aroma. But immorality or any impurity or greed must not even be named among you, as is proper among saints; and there must be no filthiness and silly talk, or coarse jesting, which are not fitting, but rather giving of thanks. For this you know with certainty, that no immoral or impure person or covetous man, who is an idolater, has an inheritance in the kingdom of Christ and God.

Let no one deceive you with empty words, for be-

cause of these things the wrath of God comes upon the sons disobedience. Therefore do not be partakers with them; for you were formerly darkness, but now you are Light in the Lord; walk as children of Light (for the fruit of the Light consists in all goodness and righteousness and truth), trying to learn what is pleasing to the Lord. Do not participate in the unfruitful deeds of darkness, but instead even expose them; for it is disgraceful even to speak of the things, which are done by them in secret. But all things become visible when they are exposed by the light, for everything that becomes visible is light (Ephesians 5:1-13 NASB).*

I believe God planted me in my ministry and my life to be a fragrant offering, to walk in love, and give myself up to sacrifice and serve God. I believe I still am. Then darkness came and cut my rose off. It was all I had to offer. All my delicate pieces fell to the ground with every pink petal deliberately stepped on and smashed into the dirt. Even though part of me fell to the ground, the other part still stood tall.

But, like the stem, I was filled with thorns, bitterness, and stiffness. I got broken and cut off from my normal life, who I used to be, and all I once knew to be reality. Then I understood I wasn't just the flower; I wasn't just the remaining stem; I was the whole tree.

In my visualization, I understood my roots went deeper, so much deeper. God is not finished cultivating me. I am not done growing because a seed has been planted in me so I can bloom again. I see lots of blooms in my future—even a rose garden!

Life may come with scissors and try to cut off the

splendor that has taken a long time to grow and mature. Life may try to separate us from who we are in Christ and what we have been called to accomplish, but nothing can separate us from the love of God!

> *What shall we say about such wonderful things as these? If God is for us, who can ever be against us? Since he did not spare even his own Son but gave him up for us all, won't he also give us everything else? Who dares accuse us whom God has chosen for his own? No one—for God himself has given us right standing with himself. Who then will condemn us? No one—for Christ Jesus died for us and was raised to life for us, and he is sitting in the place of honor at God's right hand, pleading for us. Can anything ever separate us from Christ's love? Does it mean he no longer loves us if we have trouble or calamity, or are persecuted, or hungry, or destitute, or in danger, or threatened with death? (As the Scriptures say, "For your sake we are killed every day; we are being slaughtered like sheep.) No, despite all these things, overwhelming victory is ours through Christ, who loved us. And I am convinced that nothing can ever separate us from God's love. Neither death nor life, neither angels nor demons, neither our fears for today nor our worries about tomorrow—not even the powers of hell can separate us from God's love. No power in the sky above or in the earth below—indeed, nothing in all creation will ever be able to separate us from the love of God that is revealed in Christ Jesus our Lord* (Romans 8:31-39 NLT)

119

Would I let the wickedness of Emma's actions separate me from God and his will for my life?

A BOY NAMED KENDRICK

My husband and I went to this one particular restaurant about three times a week (sometimes more) where a little boy named Kendrick came in regularly selling candy. Kendrick had the biggest smile; his teeth looked way too big for a nine-year-old boy. His spiffy shirt always looked a little small, like it might have been handed down from his older brother.

He always buttoned it up to his neck. He looked like a politician and talked like one too. One night Kendrick came into the restaurant with a huge box of candy to sell. He walked up to our booth and greeted us, "Hi, my name is Kendrick."

"Well, our names are Mike and Tracy Carpenter. Nice to meet you."

"Nice to meet you." He smiled. "I'm selling candy to pay for a trip to Disneyland."

"Really?" I continued, "Is your church around here?

"Yes."

"How many boxes of candy do you have?"

"I have twelve left. I started with twenty."

"How much are they?"

"If you buy one, they are three dollars; and if you buy two, I can give them to you for five dollars."

"Wow, how many do you need to sell today?"

"As many as possible. When we sell our whole box, we get to go to Disneyland."

"Well, Kendrick, I'll take the whole box."

"What?" he exclaimed. "Thank you so much!"

Now, about every month or so, I see Kendrick with his big smile walking in to the restaurant with full-size hopes and his eyes twinkling. Sure enough, I buy the whole box but not without catching up and hearing all about his latest adventures. I get so much joy from it.

After the Emma drama, many well-meaning friends told me that I needed better boundaries in place moving forward in the future. They loved me and wanted to protect me. Contemplating what they said for a while, I felt like they wanted me to throw my walls up as high as possible. Be on the defense. Watch out! Even for Kendrick.

I did look for areas inside the Emma story where I could have made different choices. Letting Emma stay at my house or agreeing to document all the brutality are a couple of the many areas where I believe if I had made different choices, I might have been able to better protect my personal space.

As I healed, I did put some healthy boundaries in place to protect my personal space, my time with God, and pastoral counseling time. I had to figure out how to move forward with my new borders but not with walls between myself and God and walls between others and myself. I could have easily put my fences up sky high. I could have effortlessly been defensive and cynical, but I could have missed the joy.

NINJA WARRIOR ROCKS

A few months after the Emma scandal came out in the open and died down, after I cleared my mind, broke through the fear, and heard God with clarity again, I went on one of my regular walks. That's where I hear the clearest from God, aside from the porch swing. I hiked about halfway along my regular trek.

This long paved road dead ends in a beautiful view of a quite large mountain. As you approach the end, you walk on a large bridge which was built over a sandy wash bed. A dirt trail leads up the mountain and takes you to a lookout spot. Lots of people park their cars on the bridge right before the concrete turns into dirt. They hike the dirt trail and go up to the plateau. I usually make my way to the end of the bridge, then turn around and make my way home.

I had just turned around to make my way back when a van pulled up. The family inside began spilling out all over. Do all these kids belong to this one family? Finally, a young boy got out of the van, and he jumped down super excited. They parked right on the bridge, and he made his way to the sidewalk right outside his van door.

He immediately saw the big water canal below him. He started yelling to his sister, "Kaylor, Kaylor, come look, I see ninja warrior rocks!" He kept saying it over and over. I watched how the family completely tuned him out. They busied themselves unloading and getting all the kids ready for the day's outing. I tuned in and couldn't keep my eaves-dropping ears away.

I am not sure if it's the children's pastor in me, the writer in me, or just plain little kid in me, but I was taken aback. He looked and sounded so passionate and cute. He saw what he hoped to find. I gazed down too, looking for ninja warrior rocks. At first I just saw a big ditch in front of me, but I didn't let myself off the hook. What else might I see if I looked harder for it?

I stared out over the ditch and took the time to clear my mind. Then I saw a haven for someone to hide, a place for animals to live, a place for water to run, and so on.

Sometimes I look for aches and pains and terrifying trauma that might come to find me hiding from it. I look for the reasons not to do something rather than the reasons to charge ahead. I look to the past and not the future—but that isn't how I want to live.

I had big decisions to make in the months following Emma's huge betrayal. I had to decide whether to focus on what Emma did to my family and me or focus on something bigger and brighter. I could look for darkness and see shadows everywhere. Or I could choose to look for something else.

I chose to look for something else.

I remember some years ago, I had a word from the Lord. H said, "Don't search for glass in the sand. If you search long enough in the sand, you will find a piece of glass." I am so sick of searching for glass in the sand. I bet if I looked for ninja warrior rocks, I would find them. God tried to show me how to begin looking for what I hoped to find and not what I didn't want to find. He tried to show me the power of our thoughts and how if we look for something long enough we will find it. If we seek God with all of our heart and mind, we will find him.[33]

I have decided to start looking for justice, kindness, new visions from God, laughter, and the good things little happy moments bring. I will no longer look to the past to what used to be; I will look toward the future and watch with eyes of anticipation for what new thing God will do. Isaiah 43:18-19 says, "Forget the former things; do not dwell on the past. See, I am doing a new thing!"

I am going to call my good things my ninja warrior rocks from now on! When I get tempted to search for glass, and worry sets in, he shall cover me—after a mammogram, your child out driving on New Year's Eve, a family member suffering from a serious illness. I can choose to run to the beach, and I am sure to find bottles and bottles. No more. I will run to God and find ninja warrior rocks!

I will keep my eyes on God and not be shaken.[34]

CATCH A GLIMPSE OF GLORY

We have all heard the cliché, "The eyes are the windows to the soul." It sure seems to be true, doesn't it? The love inside of us can easily be seen through our eyes and the eyes of others. Through our eyes, our tears emerge, compassion is shown, and joy and laughter are expressed. Even a simple glance can be very complicated.

When I used to drop my kids off at school, they looked back at me for a split second and, after some reflection, a profound understanding of love enveloped me. I believe God gave me spiritual wisdom and helped me to see the world from his point of view. "Your eye is a lamp that provided light for your body. When your eye is good, your whole body is filled with light" (Matthew 6:22). He allowed me some brief but beautiful moments, which have forever changed how I look at a simple glance.

It first happened one morning as my daughter walked into kindergarten. She quickly said goodbye. Her cute little bob haircut flew to the side as she grabbed her Disney backpack and made her way up the walk toward her elementary classroom. She walked about halfway toward her destination, and then she turned her head and looked back at me. At first I waved goodbye again, then after it happened day after day, I began to see so much more in her simple glimpse back.

I began to wait for it every morning. Sure enough, almost every morning she began her journey toward her day and just when you thought she wasn't going to, she looked back. As time went on, and my son grew to school age, sure enough, he looked back also. Every day just when I gave up hope and figured his days of looking back had ended, in an instant, he turned around and looked back at me. I still cherish those moments. As my children made their way to adulthood, they consistently looked for me and, to this day, still look back.

I can't help but ponder all the times I looked back. I think about all the moments I looked for my mom and dad. Sick at school as a child, I waited fervently to see my mom's face come through the door. I can see all the times my parents sat in the audience, and I peeked out behind the curtains to look for them. I still see them carrying hot dogs or drinks toward me as I sat at different sporting events.

I remember as a child waiting for them to come into my room and tuck me in every night. My eyes were fixed on the doorway. I even measured the sides of the wall every night and tried to visually mark exactly where I thought their eyes might be when they turned the corner to see me. I stared at that spot until they appeared.

It may seem like the simplest of gestures to see someone look back, but for me, a simple glance opened the floodgates to a whole new world of precious love encounters. It's funny because it's not the look or gaze that unlocks the love, is it? It is sacrifice, commitment, trust, and an intimate bond between people, which is communicated in a brief second.

Sometimes when we will take a moment, slow down, and allow God to move, he will increase our capacity to appreciate and recognize him. God has a plan, and often we are invited into that plan, which is an awesome thing. His plan has hope, purpose, blessing, promotion, validation, anointing, and a future plan inside of it.

If we can take our masks off for a short time and see into the spiritual, we will see windows open! We can see our future full of hope and void of pain. We have all heard the scripture about ears to hear and eyes to see.[35] Those who listen, look deeper, and seek God and his true leading can catch glimpses of it.

He will give us the eyes to see mercy, grace, favor, blessing, and true love all around us. I have learned to take simple moments and look back at him. I believe that when God sees us, his children, look for him during all of the moments of our journey, it must warm his heart. It is so comforting to know he is always there, waiting for us to look back and trust him, see his sacrifice, and count on him for all of our many needs.

When the glimpses of God's glory began to shine through, I truly began to heal.

JUMP

I always felt like I was in an airplane with all my fear gear on, ready to jump out but never having the courage to jump. My bags hung there stuffed with bitterness, past pain, lost hopes, and grief. I knew they couldn't go with me when I took the huge plunge—my grip firmly on the door holding on to the safety. I choose not to jump. Jumping was dangerous. Then finally, I set my bags down, said a prayer, and trusted God to guide me down safely. Sometimes we must simply let go and let God. Fear is a dirty liar. God can handle the weight of our baggage, and he can provide the parachute to ensure a safe landing.

I mentally jumped, and to my surprise, my parachute opened! I soared through the air free falling. I started screaming like one of those funny home videos where people bungee jump in the chairs, and you see them shrieking. In a couple of seconds, as I let go, I began to float down, finally getting to see the beauty in the scenery. I saw the big picture right in front of me. The ironic part is the beauty existed in the scenery all along.

Sometimes we focus so hard on holding on to the past, our tight grip keeps us from letting go and seeing it.

TWELVE

DEMONS IN MY HOUSE?

Do you remember learning to ride a bike? The big day arrived, and the training wheels came off. Excitement filled the air. Maybe one of your parents, an older sibling or a friend ran beside you. They held on to the seat or the side of the bike while you pedaled as fast as you thought possible.

You finally got some momentum and began to balance, and they took their hands away. I eventually learned how to ride my two-wheel bike, but I crashed so hard when my mom took her hands away that first time. I remember over and over colliding with the ground. Before I figured how to do it, my knee bled, tears streamed down my face, and I desperately wanted my training wheels back. My mom knew the pain was going to be short-lived. She knew I would eventually pedal long enough, and like so many before me, sail down the road riding my bike.

I see Jesus running alongside me as I ride this bike called life. He says, "Pedal faster. I have you. You can do this!" I pedal and pedal and begin to balance and get some momentum, and in a millisecond, I am tending my wounds. I think, *Why did you let go? I wasn't ready. How could you let go?*

He says, "Let's try again. You can do this!"

"No way! I am too hurt already!" He gets beside me, and

I see how tight his hands are on my seat. "Okay, I'll try again." I start pedaling so hard and fast until I realize he isn't holding me. My faith wavers, my fear swells, and down I go. We start again and again until I am really riding my bike, living my life boldly, and I see God clapping and smiling and celebrating my faith.

He is right beside me. I say, "Jesus, you were right. I could do this." It's not long before I am yelling, "Look, Jesus, no hands!" God never leaves us.[36] God will not have us do anything without his support. Sometimes the things God may be asking us to do while trusting him seem unreasonable and impossible. Forgiveness is one of those difficult things God asks us to do. Forgiving Emma required great faith and fast pedaling.

WHY?

The truth is this: Suffering comes in all shapes and sizes. No one is exempt. It can happen for all different reasons, at any given moment, in any walk of life. We can bring it on ourselves and suffer for something we have done. Other times we are victimized for something someone else did to us.[37]

We learn big lessons in life through adversity. God may permit suffering so we can learn lessons on compassion, perseverance, grace, and obedience.[38] At times, God may even allow our suffering so we can speak out through our lives to others struggling with the same things.[39]

Why did all this bad stuff happen to me? Was this just life? Did I bring this misery on myself somehow? Is there something God wants to teach me? Was I supposed to learn something? Was I supposed to inspire others with this terrible story? What is God's higher purpose in this? When we get hurt, we want to blame ourselves, our circumstances, other people, God, and sometimes, even Satan. Who do I blame?

ARE THERE DEMONS IN MY HOUSE

Emma talked like a six-year-old, had many demonic stories, stayed awake all night, and sought to take me down. At the time, it concerned me to see Emma acting so erratically. I chalked it up to the degree and type of abuse in her memories along with the medication she was taking. After I found out she faked everything, I began to wonder if her changes in demeanor and out-of-her-mind behavior signified an evil possession.

Who does what she did to us? Someone evil? It sure wasn't lovely and pure. How do we distinguish between a psychological disorder and a demon? When the truth surfaced, I speculated whether or not demonic forces influenced Emma. Did Satan himself guide and lead her? Did multiple demons take up residence in her? Was she possessed? Or was she just plain mentally ill?

Since I was a pastor working in a church and doing full-time ministry, the idea of her being possessed by demons left me feeling disturbed, fearful, and at times, stupid. I can't worry that a demon will pop out at me every time I turn around. I had nightmares and all kinds of what felt like demonic things going on around me during and after the Emma thing.

In fifteen years of ministry, where I saw plenty of abysmal trials, I never felt the need or knew to pray demons out of my house. So after this happened, people kept asking whether we have had our house prayed over. No. Should I have? Maybe each morning, it should have been a ritual like brushing my teeth just to be sure. Maybe I should have studied this more? Maybe this is my fault?

So I called a couple of pastors I knew who do this kind of prayer. When they came over and prayed demons out of my house, I sat there stunned. Couldn't I pray the demons out of my own house? Why would demons even be in my home? Jesus is in me, so how would demons get in my home? How scary is that? I guess when I went through Bible College, learning about demons didn't turn out to be my major.

This was such a dark time, and such dark issues surrounded all of Emma's lies. I wondered, *Did I not have my mind on the things of God? Did I do something to open the door to the enemy?* My brain went into a vice grip.

I have attended charismatic churches and non-denominational churches. Before I start talking about demons in any more depth, for the sake of not freaking anyone out, I made the following list of a few things I believe:

- There is only one God, the God revealed in the Bible (Deuteronomy 6:4; Romans 3:30).

- All Scripture is inspired by God and is profitable for teaching, for reproof, for correction, for training in right-eousness; that the person of God may be adequate, equipped for every good work (2 Timothy 3:16-17).

- In the beginning God created the heavens and the earth (Genesis 1:1).

- The Law is our tutor to lead us to Jesus, the Messiah (Galatians 3:24).

- Jesus of Nazareth is the Christ, the Son of the living God, and Lord. He is the image of the invisible God who came to show us what God is like and to take our sins as His on the cross so we can be saved by His sacrifice (John 1:1, 1:18; Colossians 1:16; John 3:16; 1 Peter 2:22-24).

- The Holy Spirit convicts the world of sin, self-righteousness, and judgment (John 16:8).

- People are saved by faith in Jesus because of God's grace (John 1:12; Ephesians 2:8-10).

- Anyone in Christ is a new creation (2 Corinthians 5:17).

- God wants His children to mature toward becoming like Jesus in attitudes and actions (Ephesians 4:11-5:1).

- God wants all His children to live in unity with one another (John 17:20-21) and to love one another as Jesus modeled for us (John 13:34-35; Ephesians 3:14-4:6).

- The Church is the Family of God, the Bride of Christ, the Body of Christ to continue the Father's love (Ephesians 4:14-19), the Spirit's fruit (Galatians 5:22-23), and the Son's service for mankind (John 20:21; Matthew 20:26-28; Matthew 28:19-20).

With all that said, I don't have an equal list of what I believe about demons and Satan. Or at least I did not at the time. Do you? Sometimes Christians tend to blame Satan for everything, and it's not even really him. I think evil is evil and don't discount it in any way, but I also don't want to give Satan glory for anything. I believe in Jesus. I prefer to spend more time talking about him than I do Satan.

First John 4:1 talks about discerning spirits. Was I supposed to discern this and missed it? I hope not. It may surprise you to learn that when Emma started her alter ego as a six-year-old child, I re-read everything on testing the spirits. But so did she. I found out later she had all my notes on it. She studied them just as hard as I did. Frankly, she pretended whatever she wanted. I will never be sure exactly what motivated Emma to do what she did to our family. What I can be sure of is God wins! God never left me, and I know God reigns in my home.

As I have said before, I think we find what we are looking for. I did have people pray over my home. I prayed prayers of cleansing and authority as often as possible, and I took my authority back. I don't think there is a perfect answer or regimen. I think being inundated with questions after such a tragedy is normal.

I know for sure that being a Christian is not about rules and regulations; it's about a personal relationship with Christ, our faith, and his grace. Did I need to forgive myself for being some kind of bad pastor that let demonic forces oppress me? I did not do that. If I missed something, I missed something. When we care deeply for people, sometimes our emotions can cloud our judgment. I am okay with that. I would rather be emotionally connected and authentic with others than be fake and protected.

God sees me and has called me to reach out to the lost, and when and if I make a mistake, God is right there to forgive and restore me. I decided to give God the glory for who he is and give myself a break.

ENCOURAGE PEOPLE. THEY NEED IT.

Emma's lies came out on Easter Sunday, and I took one week off from work to mentally deal with them. The week they scheduled me to come back, our whole staff planned to attend a conference in another city. My team, now shattered, struggled with this. Before the Emma drama, we all looked forward to spending these few days together, and now we didn't even want to attend. I remember trying to pack and breaking down almost the whole time.

At this conference, I saw the whole church staff team for pretty much the first time since the discovery of Emma's plot. It was a three-day conference, and in those three days, only a few people from my whole staff even spoke to me. A couple of co-workers asked some questions about the details surrounding Emma's folly and seemed in shock.

Many of the pastors just walked by me over and over again, never even nodding or saying hello. I sat close to the floor and near the aisle, which made me easily accessible as everyone made their way back from breaks and mealtime. They acted like they didn't see me, as if I didn't exist. My heart sank, and my grief intensified each time they walked past me, saying nothing.

When tragedy hits hard, you unwillingly discover who your friends are. Some of the people I revered as my greatest supporters ended up to be the exact ones who caused me more pain. The ones I expected to reach out in love and be sensitive to my situation were the exact ones who chose to ignore me, and in some cases, even avoid me for months after the revelation of Emma's deceit.

The first day I returned to work, memories of Emma seemed to be all over my office. I sat alone in my desk chair and replayed thousands of moments. I glanced around my office, and it seemed stripped bare. I felt cold, older, and not wiser. My husband called to check on me a few times. Numbness strangled me. I wanted to leave; I wanted to go home. I wanted to be anywhere but in the office where all of this started.

So many of the girls I worked with quit, and their empty spaces haunted me. I missed them. I missed my old life. Confusion and grief filled my days as I struggled to work. I had to go through all of her drawers, where I found notes she wrote about me. I had to clear her computer, and I found she sent some of the Owen emails from my very own computer.

Each day new proof of her treachery and dishonesty fell right in my lap. Co-workers avoided me in the hall or turned their heads when they saw me. Tears never left my eyes. I am not sure why they ignored me. Numerous days I felt as if I carried a deadly disease. This left me baffled. I remember thinking, *Do they think I'm not spiritual enough? Do they think I did something to cause this? Do they wish I would just quit?* I didn't quit.

Other people whom I thought didn't really know me very well or care that much, brought food, left me notes, and continued to pray and check in on me. I am deeply grateful for those who stepped out, stood up, and did something for me. I needed it.

Whenever something of this magnitude hits a church, all the same conversations begin to take place. Publicly, it's all about protecting the church and Emma. Remember her parents attended and gave to this church. Privately, it's an archeology experiment where everyone is trying to find out what really happened. Then it turned to prevention. These are not bad things. I just wished for more benevolence.

I know with all my heart no one intentionally set out to hurt me. I know people are not perfect. I know the church is full of imperfect people—heck, I'm one of them. I know God loves his church, and the church is a wonderful place for people to find transformation in Jesus. I believe in the church.

I know if someone had died in my family, my counter would have been full of food. This situation broke the rules. This situation didn't play fair. This situation carried with it a taboo. Emma threatened the church, her lies involved the church, and her actions were in opposition to the church.

The main idea, which my management continued to communicate to me, looked like this: let's just forget this, never speak of it (to protect Emma's family and the church), and move on. It sounded great to me but felt awful.

It seemed the risk and the professional side of things outweighed the personal side. I heard a lot of, "How will you prevent this from happening again in the future?" and "How will you pull a team together to get back on track?" I get it. I am in leadership and have had years of experience in my role. What I failed to hear, "How are you?" "We care about you!" "How are you doing?" "I am so sorry this happened to you." "Is there anything I can do?" "Just checking in on you." Somewhere along the way, what Emma did overshadowed what she did to me.

I believe we who serve the church in ministry need to offer grace to people, no matter what the circumstance. God loves homosexuals, drug addicts, and cheaters. He also loves people who are hurting, no matter why they are hurting. He still loves them. In fact, he died for them. I believe we must work harder at letting go of our fears, insecurities, and judgments and just plain reach out in love to hurting people. I know I will.

I had expectations, which I believe were in right alignment with God and his Word. However, those same expectations taught me to put expectations on God, not people. I came away with an important lesson—I will never sit on the sidelines again. I hope you won't either. When people are suffering, I will step up and encourage them because they need it.

When people have to miss work for a week because they are broken, I will encourage them because they need it. I won't ignore suffering people because I don't know what to say, or their situation is a touchy subject. I will encourage them. They need it. I know firsthand they need it.[40]

Part of the healing process for me, and I believe you too, includes accepting the fact that our choices are not always going to make sense to everyone. Only God knows the inner workings of our hearts. We must forgive and let go of the hurt and expectations we place on people because we often have enough hurt for all of them. If we sow anger, bitterness, and resentment into our hearts, then surely ugly weeds will soon spring up and begin to choke out any healthy thing trying to grow through our lives.

I had to release it all to God and allow him to work through my situation where he eventually brought healing and a sound perspective.

People's imperfections don't define God's greatness.

THIRTEEN

FORGIVENESS IS FREEDOM

I led devotions for our staff meeting some months after I began healing from the Emma torment. I like to choose a topic that is true to me. So I chose the verse Luke 6:28: "Bless those who curse you, pray for those who mistreat you."

I chose that verse because someone else had been especially unkind to me. They hurt my feelings; I did not want to get caught up being offended but wanted to re-align my focus. I began studying, and then as I made notes and started preparing for my devotion, I began to dive into these verses:

> Bless those who persecute you; bless and do not curse. Rejoice with those who rejoice; mourn with those who mourn. Live in harmony with one another. Do not be proud, but be willing to associate with people of low position. Do not be conceited. Do not repay anyone evil for evil. Be careful to do what is right in the eyes of everyone. If it is possible, as far as it depends on you, live at peace with everyone. Do not take revenge, my dear friends, but leave room for God's wrath, for it is written: "It is mine to avenge; I will repay," says the Lord. On the contrary "If your enemy is hungry, feed him; if he is thirsty, give him

*something to drink. In doing this, you will heap
burning coals on his head. Do not be overcome by
evil, but overcome evil with good* (Romans 12:14-21).

I immediately forgot about this other person, and the
Spirit took my mind straight to Emma. I felt God trying to tell
me something. Surely he knew it was too soon for me to get
over what she had done to me. This sounded pretty radical.

Deep inside I felt downright hateful toward her. Anger
and revenge encapsulated my heart. Bitterness filled my
soul. I wanted her to get what was coming to her. Bless
Emma? Pray for Emma? Wish her well? No way. I wanted
her to suffer. I wanted her to be punished for what she did.

I had thought I had forgiven a sick girl for what she did
on the premise of her probably not knowing what she was
doing.[41] What I didn't do, nor did I want to do, was pray for
her to get great things and hope that her life would become
awesome. I didn't want to see Emma the way God sees her. I
wanted to see her the way I saw her. In those moments, I
felt convicted. In those powerful moments, I began to put
new lenses on and look at Emma the way God might.

She mattered to God, and he called me to love her. Love
her? Was he kidding me? I already tried that—and look
where it got me. Then the scriptures I did know about
vengeance and God vindicating people came straight to my
heart. God has his job, and he does the punishing. My job is
to do what? You guessed it, trust God again. It wasn't about
me forgiving Emma as much as my obedience to God. Then
you add in all the scripture about my prayer life being inhib-
ited if I hold any forgiveness in my heart. Uh-oh. I wanted
my prayers answered.

Surely, God knew it wasn't possible for me to wish her

well. I wanted her to get the help she needed. I didn't want her happy because she didn't deserve it. She proved to be a very dangerous person with no conscience. She didn't deserve to be laughing it up with a great life.

She deserved to be found out, and all her dark plots on people to be discovered. She deserved to be prosecuted. I am not like her! Emma and I were polar opposites. For example, I exist to help people, and she exists to hurt people. I tell the truth; she lies. I give; she takes. I cherish my friends; she doesn't know the meaning of friendship.

Then God let me know in the way he does, as tears gushed down my face, I don't deserve it either. My quiet moments did not get spent thinking about how God feels about Emma. My quiet moments stayed full of thoughts about how I felt about what Emma did. I guess I thought God felt what I felt. I don't set out to betray and hurt people. I don't lie and make up fake stories to damage people's lives. Then I truly grasped that it just doesn't matter what she did; it matters what God did. The Holy Spirit let me know she does deserve it. God died on a cross for her. God loves Emma. I needed to let go of my bitterness.

Letting go of my pain, resentfulness, and distaste proved difficult. If I were going to become more like Christ, I must find a way to love Emma too. Mary Demuth says in her book *Everything,* "Our task shouldn't be punishing the villains in our lives, but enlarging the God who heals us from all wounds." Ugh. So, as hard as it was, I began to picture her doing well. I began to pray for her life. I disagree with what she did. Some days I still hurt over the pain she caused.

It is one thing to remember God is there. It's quite another to believe he is there for us! God is my healer, and

God was my provision and provider. God is the lifter of my head (Psalm 3:3 NIV).

No matter how difficult it might become, I knew I needed to step out in faith and trust God to work this out. He loved her, but I also recognized he did not love what she did to me. It seemed hard for me to separate those two things at first. I had to let go of my bitterness and let him do the punishing. Letting go of all that junk wasn't the burden I expected. I felt honored to give it up.

Truthfully, it felt good. I got so inspired that I began searching my heart for anything else I might be holding onto. I hadn't forgiven those who were responsible for misdiagnosing my mom. I hadn't truly forgiven those in South Dakota for hurting me. God and I have had some pretty meaningful conversations.

I decided not to blame Emma, my circumstances, Satan, or myself for what happened. I decided to get into alignment with the Lord and choose to forgive and focus on not staying offended and not getting caught up in the mud of that. I decided to let go of my anger. "Anger is extraordinarily easy. It's our default setting. Love is very difficult. Love is a miracle."[42]

ARE YOU A STUMP?

One of my favorite books is *The Giving Tree* by Shell Silverstein. I often give it to people as a gift. It's a great story about a tree and a little boy. The story encapsulates years, and over the years, the tree offers everything she has to the boy. The story starts when the boy is young. As the boy grows up, he continues to return to the tree, and the tree continues to offer all she has to him. The tree loves the boy.

She gives him apples to eat, branches to swing on, and even her trunk when he needs it.

I have read lots of ideas and perspectives from different people on the meaning of this book. Some see the boy as a selfish boy; some see the tree as a loving tree. Some see the tree as passive; some the tree as radically generous. For quite a few years, I looked at the story of *The Giving Tree* like this: The boy kept returning as he grew up, and each time he came back to the loving tree he just took. The tree had so much to give out of love, and she just gave and gave until she had nothing left to give to anyone else. Because she continued to give everything away, she became a stump, with nothing left to give to others.

After the Emma stuff, I identified myself with the stump: She took all my apples, branches, and the trunk. She even sat on my stump. I came in as a loving person willing to give all I had to help her find healing and true happiness. And she took and took and took. I felt cut down with nothing left to give to others.

If you're familiar with the story, you know at the end of each outpouring of the tree, it says, "The tree was happy." The tree was happy after she gave her apples, branches, trunk, and her stump. I think I looked at it all wrong all of these years. In the past, people have taken advantage of my generosity—people only wanting more, taking and not giving anything in return. When this happens, I often related it to this story. I gave so much over and over, especially to one person, it quickly made me into the stump. I didn't want to be a stump anymore because I felt like those who took advantage of my generosity left no apples for those who had the ability to appreciate the gesture and the fruit I had to offer. This could limit my generosity for sure.

But if I shift my emphasis just a touch and not focus on the stump, I saw the tree was happy. Sure the boy could have been more grateful; he could have left something for someone else. Nevertheless, the tree was happy to sacrifice. The truth is I too felt happy to sacrifice, and the beauty is I don't feel like a stump anymore. I focused on the giving, not the taking.

In the same way, look at all the people for whom God sacrificed. He gave his only Son's life and made the most ultimate sacrifice, and for what? He sacrificed his Son so we can all be forgiven. If we are to become more like Christ, at times, we too must make the ultimate sacrifice to forgive as well. Sometimes we can see it like we are the stump when we give out of undeserved, radical sacrificial generosity.

In reality, the tree trunk had been sacrificed for the boy and provided a seat for an old man to rest. When the tree thought it had nothing left to offer, it still did. When it came time to forgive Emma, others, God, and myself, I wasn't sure it would even be possible. I felt as if all my apples, branches, and trunk were gone. I felt like an old stump.

The discovery for me is that happiness can be found in offering all I have left. Because of Jesus, I get to give as well as be forgiven, and in the end, I become more like him. The great part is I am growing again, and soon I will have many more apples to give, branches to share, and trunk to chop down to provide for someone who needs it.

You may feel as if you're a stump. Maybe you gave all of your apples to someone in hopes of helping them only to be taken advantage of. Maybe you have been holding onto forgiveness for those who have raided your trees. Make a decision today to sacrifice, and when it seems your sacrifice brought you pain or just doesn't feel worth it, think about the tree and not the boy. When we let go of unforgiveness, we are free. We can find new levels of compassion and grace. Balance and wholeness can invade our lives when we are open to new people and new relationships. When we stand ready to give and to offer ourselves kindly, it not only connects us to one another but it connects us deeply with Christ.

With each sacrifice of forgiveness, I can and will be happy. And so can you! The tree was happy, and so am I.

FOURTEEN

A HANDWRITTEN LIFE

Living life in cursive is my metaphor for staying connected to the things in life which keep us whole, balanced, and full of beauty. When we embrace all the letters that make us who we are and connect them to the passions, personalities, and people in our lives, we become full expressions of our unique character. When we live our lives in cursive through sharing creativity, learning perseverance, living out our faith, telling our stories, accepting our weaknesses, and ultimately finding our strengths, our lives shine brightly back at us with beautiful penmanship.

Have you ever tried to write with a feather pen? This is the type of pen where you insert the feather quill into a nib and then dip the tip of the nib into an ink jar and begin writing. It's no easy task, for it takes patience. Flat worn spots and skipping of the ink on the paper are just a couple of things that may happen.

This type of writing instrument needs to be cleaned, soaked, blotted, and even re-inked. It is super sensitive to force, pressure, and speed. But there are also advantages to the feather pen. The ink can be more waterproof and permanent than ballpoint pens. Feather pens have unique line patterns so that you can make different strokes with them that can appear wider or thinner.

Writing with a feather pen can be messy, especially if it breaks. The marvelous thing is when the feather pen is working properly so that the ink breaks through the way it is supposed to do, it is a lovely thing to see. The writing is smooth, creative, individual, personal, and memorable.

I feel a little like this feather pen. Writing or living is no easy task; it takes patience. Catastrophes happen in life. Tragedies may threaten to break our quills, stop us from writing, and leave us stained with the aftereffects of the misfortune. We too need to be cleaned up, soaked, blotted, and especially re-inked. I am so sensitive to pressure and force. The harder some things get, the more mess I seem to be in.

Life in Christ can protect us and make us more waterproof. My life especially has such unique line patterns. When Emma began her betrayal, I believe my life served as a beautiful longhand expression of my beliefs, my love of God, and my heart for humanity. Then as I continued to live my life in a flowing and picturesque way, my quills unexpectedly broke and spattered all over me.

Sometimes when things get broken, we need to try to fix what broke; other times, we must discard the item and find a new one. Sometimes we clean it up, and sometimes we throw it in the trash, never needing a replacement. All of this happening right in the middle of my life and ministry got messy; I did not wish for this suffering on my birthday when I blew out the candles.

Immediate clean up became necessary. I needed a breakthrough.

I hear all the time how "I need a breakthrough" or "I need to break the strongholds in my life." I learned from my own experience that what we really need is help to heal what has been broken first, and then we can get through to a new beginning or a fresh place of freedom. God has break-throughs waiting for us.

I see it like the line at the fabric store. If you have ever gone in to buy fabric, you take a little ticket and wait and watch each person step up to get their fabric cut. Soon your number is called, and then you step up and get your fabric cut. We must wait and be patient. We can't barge up to the counter, pushing our way forward.

After the initial pain, God sees we are still holding fabric, and he is just waiting with what we need, but we have to follow the right steps if we ever want to see that counter. A true breakthrough doesn't come in one quick step. I found that God's sudden breakthroughs were never sudden at all. They came after a very long time of trying to understand. Some of my greatest breakthroughs came from years of praying, studying, and living my life in Christ. Then suddenly, all my past experiences, learning, and God's words came to-gether through mind-bending breakthroughs to free me!

Throughout my journey of learning to live my life in cur-sive following the heartbreaking events I endured, break-throughs came right and left, just none of them in one quick second. I had to re-focus and look only for Jesus. I had to re-mind myself repeatedly that the Holy Spirit is in me, and Satan has no power over me.[43]

I had to take baby steps and stay in constant contact with God. I let go of my fears and bitterness and clung to God. I still do. I spent hours reading the Bible and through my journals, and God's words began to jump off the pages, especially the words on forgiveness and trusting him. I lis-tened closely for his voice and his voice only. If ever I had a question, I went back to the basics and tried to do nothing on my own initiative. I got to know Jesus better, and with the help of the Holy Spirit, continued and am continuing to become more like him.[44]

I see now how willing God is to work through our messy situations and, in his timing, give us new understanding and complete healing. We must be willing to surrender everything to him, and then he will provide us with our much desired and needed breakthrough.

This whole nightmare molded my perspective of God, gave me a whole new outlook on life, and taught me what I believe to be valuable lessons: Maybe my lessons can be your lessons.

Here they are:

- I can't be everything to everybody. I can't even be everything to myself. The only one who can be everything is the one who is everything, and that is Jesus.

- When a tragedy hits someone I know, even if I don't understand why I will reach out and show compassion and encourage him or her.

- I will choose hope and simply choose to believe in God's provision no matter what circumstances present themselves.

- I may not always hear God perfectly. I will test the spirits and wait on God to reveal his truth through any words he gives me.

- I will not get offended. I will never understand where people are in their lives, and it is not my job to judge them for what they do or don't do.

- I will let God convict those who hurt me.
- I will pray for those who have cursed me to be blessed, even when it is hard.
- I will forgive those who have hurt me.
- I am not going to base my decisions on my fear.
- God loves his church.
- People are broken and selfish and, at times, those people will hurt me.
- I will not put grace in a box.
- I will look for open doors, not stare at closed ones.
- I am just as guilty as anyone else.
- His yoke is easy, and his burden is light.
- I can trust God with my fears and concerns (1Peter 5:7, Phillip 4:6-7).
- I will not seclude myself. God made us to be in relationship with others (Genesis 2:18).
- I will not engage in bitterness and self-pity.
- Patience brings perseverance. I will wait on God (Psalm 27:14).
- God is good all the time.
- My joy is not dependent upon my circumstances (Habakkuk 3:16-19).
- I will not sacrifice my alone time with God to serve God.

Some time ago, I read a book called *The Kite Runner* by Khaled Hosseini. What a great story of guilt, redemption, love, sacrifice, beauty, and ashes. One quote in the book that has forever stuck with me is, "For you a thousand times over." This quote appears to me often like a flashing motel sign in the middle of the night. It resonates deeply with me because it means knowing the consequences of what this situation of Emma brought me and the implications of what followed, I would do it again. It means knowing the pain and heartache, the grief and doubt, the guilt, redemption, love, sacrifice, beauty, and ashes, I would do it again if it would bring me to where I am today—right in the center of God's will, safe, and saved.

INFREQUENT PEN LIFTING

Those who want to write in cursive exquisitely must study the letters of the alphabet. To live our lives exquisitely in cursive, we must study God's Word.

Our lives bring so many priorities, commitments, responsibilities, and brutal challenges. Some of us are running kids everywhere, supervising homework, cooking dinner, organizing bills, and balancing family pressures. Others are working full-time jobs, which require commuting to faraway places, and even more of us are caught up in the daily grind.

Some are going through a difficult season, fighting an illness, grieving a loved one, or trying to find their way through a bitter trauma. So many significant things call for our attention and devotion: our kids, our husbands or wives, our jobs, and sometimes even our hobbies. We must be careful not to let our commitments and responsibilities become more important than our relationship with God. We can't let anything disconnect us.

With all of the demands and distractions before us, it can be almost impossible to establish a habit of living for God. Today's culture has brought all kinds of competition for our attention; more and more single moms and dads are trying to do everything. And it doesn't matter what our family unit looks like. Trying to find an opportunity for quality time with God can be very challenging.

During the months I dealt with Emma, I had a hard time focusing on God, reading the Word, and finding quiet time. Her life swallowed my life. If life didn't already have enough chores and responsibilities, it sure has distractions. We are inundated with the latest technology. Not only are we influenced by the mass media, but also we are entertained by the world.

We are extremely attached to media technologies such as the computer, internet, instant messaging, social networking websites, virtual reality games, automated learning devices, mobile phones, text messaging, YouTube, and all sorts of computerized handheld technology. For us to sit quietly and hear from God, stay united with him, and communicate with him can be very challenging.

His Word can bring peace and rest to our spirits. His Word can help us to direct our attention and priorities toward the right direction. His Word can teach us boundaries and balance. His Word can give us inspiration for any dilemma we may be facing. His Word can be our safe haven in the whirlwind of our lives. God can be our strong tower and our best friend!

When we choose to serve God with our whole heart and put God first in our lives, we are sure to be full of joy and peace. We can let the word of God renew our minds and direct our every step.[45] We can hear God's voice spoken directly to us through his Word. Bible reading isn't a chore or a checklist. Reading the Bible can connect us to God's thoughts, and we can truly live in unison with his ways just by spending time with him.

THE QUICK BROWN FOX JUMPS OVER THE LAZY DOG

One day when I went on one of my walks, I rounded a corner when a large dog came charging at me. He barked and began to chase me. I ran into a neighbor's open garage and hid behind their car. I kept trying to look to see if the dog ran away but couldn't make my way out of their garage far enough to see. I banged on the door in the garage. No one answered. I heard the dog again, and I froze.

I searched the garage for some kind of weapon to use in case he charged in to attack me. (A dog had bitten me in the past, so those memories flooded back to me.) The garage looked clean and organized. I felt like I invaded their privacy. I pictured myself jumping on top of their car if it ran at me. I found a squeegee on the shelf, and I practiced swinging it.

I banged on the door some more, yelling, "Hello, anyone in there?" I kept thinking they were going to walk out and see me in their garage holding the squeegee and think I was a prowler or something. Time passed so slowly. I could not come out of hiding. Then a woman walked up the driveway and into the garage.

"Are you okay?" she asked.

"No! A big dog came running at me, and I ran in this garage to be safe."

"This is my garage I live here."

"Oh? It was a brown dog, really big and barking at me!"

"This dog?" Then she pointed at the dog walking up the driveway.

"Yes!" I continued, "Is he nice?"

"Oh....hahaha... she wouldn't hurt a fly."

"Phew, I was so scared!" I made my way slowly out of the garage.

"I'm so sorry!"

Put your dog on a leash, I thought and took a deep breath of relief and gave her back her squeegee. (I found out later their security cameras in the garage taped my whole embarrassing moment.) I came out of hiding and finished up my day and my walk.

Things continue to happen in my life where I initially run and hide as a defense mechanism. For me it's a bad habit. Fear is my first reaction to when my husband cuts his hand at work, my son is in a car accident, and I find a lump on my body. Off I go running, looking for a safe place and weapon. There is this song I love by Steffany Gretziner called "Out of Hiding." I love how she sings so beautifully that we can come of hiding because we're safe with him (Jesus).

So as the fear comes at me like a charging dog, my first response is to go running to hide! Instead, I have learned to throw it off and go running to God. He is my weapon.

When we can learn to trust and depend on God more, it's not that we will never feel fear, or sadness, or grief. It's not that we will never feel like we need to go hide. How could we not? I think we find God sooner and sooner and sooner in the midst.

PRACTICE MAKES PERFECT

Working in children's ministry, I routinely shopped for preschool supplies at a local learning supply company. They have something there called sentence strips. They are long wide pieces of paper with the dotted line on them. They are used for kids to practice writing in cursive. I feel that while I am now living my life in cursive again, I still need to practice staying connected to the things that matter in my life.

There is no guarantee that nothing bad will ever happen to me again. Even as I began implementing the various changes God put on my heart, opposition came over and over again. Just when I thought my fear died, something always happened to send me running. At first I felt deflated, as if I failed God.

Then I had to go right back to my tools and begin again. There is no doubt you will also face opposition when you attempt to implement change within your life. But let me assure you that God will guide you through every situation.

Did you know that "The quick brown fox jumps over the lazy dog" is a pangram? What this means is it uses every letter of the alphabet. This is an example of a sentence teachers sometimes use to help kids practice when they are learning to type or write. If they write this over and over, they get to practice using all the letters.

When something unexpected happens to me, I think of this sentence. I will use my whole arsenal of letters to practice and get better at my writing—to fight back against Satan, rest in peace, and live in victory. I must use every tool I have. I am not sure about you, but when I have no peace, I have no life.

Wherever you are on your journey, your goals are quite simple: connect with God on a personal level and live a life honoring to Him. We all want to avoid the traps of Satan, find our true purpose and calling, live a fulfilling life, serve others, disciple others, have unshakable faith, please God, and live our lives in cursive, connected to God.

If I am going to continue to live my life in cursive, I will need to grab my negative thoughts and send them back where they came from, read my Bible, go for a walk, cry, and pray. I will need to rely on the Word of God, step out in faith, and make some tough choices swiftly. I will need to forgive others and myself quickly. When the doubts and emotional torment begin to overwhelm me, I will need to choose to believe in what I know to be true, not in what I feel.

I must choose to trust God. I plan on using every good gift he has ever given me.[46] I know I can stay strong in my beliefs and keep my eyes on God.[47] I know now how vital being whole, balanced and inspired is. I know how dangerous it is to disconnect from ourselves and God. I know how incredible it feels to embrace my vulnerabilities, share my creativity, and live out my faith. I believe I have found my rhythm now, and I believe you can too. Lots of things in this life sure aren't fair. Just remember God is just.[48] We don't need to take revenge, and we don't need to lose our hope.

FIFTEEN

CHARACTER IN THE CURSIVE

Cursive is an art. It's woven into the very fabric of the U.S. Constitution. Yet everywhere we look, it's being written out of existence. We wonder, however, if amidst the back-and-forth, an important point doesn't get lost, carried out to sea with the perfectly crafted, three-story sandcastle, namely, the meaning that a handwritten message can send. Not just the aesthetics but the expression of thought. There's something to be said for reading into those jagged, curvaceous edges, interpreting the tear-soaked, bleeding splotches, or following those clean, decisive strokes just to see where they lead.[49]

Handwriting is, I believe, a visible form of a person's voice. It can include pitch (high or low levels) and tone (formal or informal, for example), and the utensil with which we write is merely a microphone. In going through all my mom's items following her death, I found a book she had once given me as a gift. It was one of those books where you fill in all the blanks as a template used to write a biography.

The book had tons of profound questions, leaving nice, roomy spaces for her to answer every question. She filled in all the blank spaces with great stories of her childhood and her biggest hopes and greatest dreams. It outlined all her favorite things and most of her major disappointments, taking her a whole year to finish it.

She worked on the book in secret, and I never knew she worked on it until I received it as a gift. She wrote every word in her unique handwriting. At the back of the book sat a blank page, and she chose to write me this long personal letter on it. The letter was set apart from the rest of the book.

Dear Tracy,

I just wanted to add a few words, unrelated to the rest of the book, about how I feel right now at this moment 2:55 p.m. I'm sitting on the patio of the La Jolla Del Cabo in San Jose Del Cabo in Baja California. I know you remember this trip. To date it is the best vacation I have ever had. I'm overlooking a beautiful pool, a sandy beach and the Sea of Cortez. It is warm and balmy, about 85 degrees. Other than feeling full (stuffed) from eating a giant hamburger at Zippers (delicious!) I probably feel as good as I have ever felt in my life. No aches, no pains, no hard breathing! I wish you were here. I wish we never had to leave. No stress, no pain. The Lord will surely pick a spot like this to appear for the rapture! I can't remember ever breathing air like this. Don't deprive yourself from this kind of joy, Tracy, or deprive your family. Don't get wrapped up in the everyday problems, but see the beauty in what God created. For it is not where we live now, but in other spots not yet spoiled by man's greed and lust. All that matters is love of God, love of each other, and peace of mind. I love you all.

Love,

Mom

When someone dies, you sift through all their possessions and your belongings, looking for something to bring
them back. You stare at old pictures, trying to remember the
good times. You listen to recordings of their voice to open
your heart to their love again. Soon after she died, I was dig-
ging through some of my stuff and found the book she had
given me. I had forgotten about it.

I plopped it open, and all her memories fascinated me,
but the letter she wrote to me spoke to my heart. I glared at
the letter, and it glared back at me. I re-read it again, this
time with her gone. Every word seemed meant for the moment I read it. I paused as I read it to take breaths and cry.
Talk about a breakthrough.

All her words spoke about heaven and things I should
never miss in this world. I wept. I believe through her hand,
the Holy Spirit took her love and his and gave me the most
treasured tangible thing I now have—her words in her handwriting.

All the letters joined together to bless me and help me
heal. I saw the fun she had that day. I felt her love for me.
She gave me a glimpse of the heaven she dreamed of. Her
character was reflected in her cursive.

My grandma left behind journals and journals of her
thoughts when she died as well. She kept a journal for most
of her life. Unlike my mom, she wrote all the time. Her
writing in the years before her death appeared crooked and
messy due to rheumatoid arthritis. I could barely make out
some of the words. I saw plainly from her journals the days
she wrote while riddled in pain.

The moments she suffered stood out. Her voice spoke to
me as she wrote about her kids and their adventures. As I

read them, I listened to hear her laugh. She had the best laugh.

Her hopes and enthusiasm became evident through her stories. Her kindness breathed new life into me every time I read them. Her character was reflected in every stroke of her hand.

BOLD AND CLEAR HAND

In 1863, when the Emancipation Proclamation was signed, Abraham Lincoln said, "I believe in this measure my fondest hopes will be realized." But, as historian Doris Kearns Goodwin explains, "as he [Abraham Lincoln] was about to put his signature on the proclamation, his own hand was numb and shaking because he had shaken a thousand hands that morning at a New Year's reception.

"So he put the pen down and said, 'If ever my soul were in an act it is in this act, but if I sign with a shaking hand, posterity will say, he hesitated.' So he waited until he could take up the pen and sign with a bold and clear hand. There's a reason Lincoln waited to sign his name. It wasn't just about the act of writing itself.

"It was about the subtleties of his signature, the strength of his hand, and the fortitude and resolve that generations would discern, in that single, sweeping script known as Abraham Lincoln. Obviously, he felt his character would be reflected, not only in his words and acts, but also in the stroke of his pen."[50]

SIGNATURE

I believe we can see the strength of God's hand, his fortitude, and the resolve that generations will discern if we will live our lives in cursive, intentionally staying connected to God.[51] I am not sure where this finds you. Do you need to fall back in love with a God you have lost touch with? You can study the letters again; you can find fresh paper and fresh ink! You can try a few sentences, and I promise you can find your rhythm with God and his voice again.

He has a purpose for you. He wants you to be whole, balanced, and to feel loved. He wants you to have peace in your heart and life. He wants to be connected to you and talk to you. If hearing from God is new to you, then I believe you can slow down and not pressure yourself.

You can find his voice and his will if you seek him. God's character is reflected in his words all through the Bible. His signature is on our hearts the moment we chose to believe and accept him and invite him into our personal lives. Have you invited him in?

I believe God's character is reflected in our signature, and our signature is how we live our lives. Will you live your life in cursive? Joining every stroke back to him, even with a shaking hand, will you commit to God's will for your life? Will you let your life be an expression of God's penmanship? Will you let him write your story? Will you stay connected to the things in life that keep you deeply secure and rooted in inspiration. Will you please write in calligraphy, leaving beauty behind on every piece of paper you get?

When the ink spills, will you promise to throw that piece of paper away and get out a new one? When your pen runs out of ink, will you please let God refill it? Don't just send notes, sign deeds, and make lists. Write sentences, chapters, and books. Scribble, draw, and doodle. Will you stay with the loops and arches and full stops? Will you let ink smudge all over your hand? Will you allow your writing to reflect authenticity in your heart? Will you let your character be reflected in every stroke of your hand?

BREAKING THE GLASS

I shattered the glass of the glass house I once lived in. I'm not going to lie and try to say I did it alone. I am not going to lie and say I didn't have chards of glass sticking out of my arms and legs and blood running down my body. The truth is and the thing that matters most is, I broke out. I found fresh air and fresh insight.

I emerged on my knees with my hands open, and frankly, I am still there. The calling on my life, the friend I know I have in Christ, and the desire I have to be continually transformed made my stay in the glass house worth every second.

I learned the value of God's heart for humanity and ultimately his heart for me. I learned how to live my life in cursive again, every letter of my life connecting back to what matters most—God.

May my character be reflected in the stroke of my hand,

NOTES

[1] 1 Peter 5:8

[2] Matthew 5:45

[3] 1 Samuel 7:12

[4] Matthew 18:3

[5] Luke 15:11-32

[6] John 10:27

[7] Isaiah 55:8

[8] 2 Corinthians 1:4

[9] John 14:2

[10] Habakkuk 2.2

[11] 1 Kings 19:12

[12] Acts 2:1-4,17

[13] Psalm 126:6

[14] Proverbs 3:6

[15] Matthew 18:24

[16] Jeremiah 29:11

[17] 1 Peter 3:18

[18] Isaiah 53:5

[19] Isaiah 53:3

[20] Joshua 1:8

[21] James 3:17

[22] James 3:14,15

[23] Psalm 46:10

[24] Matthew 6:31-32; Philippians 4:19

[25] Romans 8:28

[26] Isaiah 61:3

[27] Hebrews 13:8

[28] Isaiah 61:7

[29] 2 Corinthians 10:5

[30] Ecclesiastes 3:1

[31] Wikipedia, Helen Keller, en.wikipedia.org, https://en.wikipedia.org/wiki/Helen_Keller

[32] Lamentations 3:23

[33] Jeremiah 29:13; Deuteronomy 4:29

[34] Psalm 16:8

[35] Matthew 13:16

[36] Deuteronomy 31:6

[37] Hebrews 12:5-11

[38] Hebrews 5:8; Romans 12:1-2

[39] John 9

[40] Hebrews 10:25

[41] Luke 23:34

[42] Brant Hansen, *Unoffendable: How Just One Change Can Make All of Life Better*, W Publishing, 2015.

[43] 2 Corinthians 1:22

[44] John 5:19-20,30

[45] Psalm 119:133

[46] Matthew 7:11

[47] Psalm 119:37

[48] 2 Thessalonians 1:6

[49] Bobby and June George, "Don't Write Off Cursive," *The Atlantic*, the-atlantic.com, https://www.theatlantic.com/education/archive/2013/10/dont- write-off-cursive/280126/, October 1, 2013

[50] *Ibid*

[51] Psalm 102:18

ABOUT THE AUTHOR

TRACY CARPENTER DMIN has been a pastor for twenty years. She has been published multiple times in national magazines and produces a large array of curriculum worldwide. Presently Tracy owns "Cursive," a brick and mortar shop located in Corona, CA. Cursive is an extension of her passion to connect with others. She encourages her followers and her shoppers to seize every opportunity they get to try new things and reflect on creative ways to not only spend their time but also enrich their life with deeper joy and greater significance. She inspires people every day to live their lives in Christ and in cursive.

Tracy uses her real-life experiences to inspire and empower others to reestablish emotional and spiritual well-being during their suffering and after trauma. Tracy and her husband, Mike, have been married more than 25 years and are the parents of two children: Amanda and Adam. They have three grandchildren Silas, Briella, and Jaxon.

CONTACT INFO

You can follow Tracy Carpenter in her quest to live a handwritten life @cursive_shop or visit her at lifeincursive.com. She welcomes email at tracy@lifeincursive.com and owns a shop in Corona, CA called "Cursive."